Butterfly Gardening

To Dad —
Merry Christmas!
Love,
Beth Larry Meg
         Mike
Jeff
   Evan   Christy
Andrew.
   Allison

1994

Perched comma (*Polygonia comma*) on crab apple (Rosaceae).

Butterfly Gardening
Creating Summer Magic in Your Garden

Created by
THE XERCES SOCIETY
in association with
THE SMITHSONIAN INSTITUTION

~

Published by
SIERRA CLUB BOOKS
SAN FRANCISCO

in association with the
NATIONAL WILDLIFE FEDERATION
WASHINGTON, D.C.

Published jointly by Sierra Club Books, San Francisco, and the National Wildlife Federation, Washington, D.C.

Library of Congress Cataloging-in-Publication Data
Butterfly gardening: creating summer magic in your garden / created by the Xerces Society in association with the Smithsonian Institution.
    p.   cm.
  Includes bibliographical references.
  ISBN 0-87156-615-X
  1. Butterflies.   2. Gardening to attract wildlife.   I. Xerces Society.   II. Smithsonian Institution.
QL544.S86   1990   90-30362
595.78′9—dc20   CIP

Note on photo captions: Although in most cases we have attempted to present complete information for butterflies and plants appearing in photographs throughout this book, taxonomic identification from color transparencies (especially at the species level) is sometimes difficult. The identification of species illustrated should therefore be viewed as a best effort rather than as an absolute statement of fact.

Scientific consultants: Paul A. Opler, Managing Editor, Office of Information Transfer, U.S. Fish and Wildlife Service, Fort Collins, Colorado; Robert K. Robbins, Associate Curator of Entomology, National Museum of Natural History, Smithsonian Institution; Stanwyn G. Shetler, Curator of Botany, National Museum of Natural History, Smithsonian Institution.

Xerces Society publications editor: Mary Troychak

Editors: Linda Gunnarson and Frances Haselsteiner
Production: Susan Ristow
Text design: Paula Schlosser
Cover design: Paul Gamarello
Garden design diagrams: Mary Booth

Printed in Hong Kong by South Sea International Press, Ltd.

10   9   8   7 6   5   4   3   2

~

*For Paul A. Opler, whose invaluable expertise,
steadfast support, and unflagging good humor
sustained us in our efforts to create this book*

The Xerces Society

was established in 1971 as a non-profit organization dedicated to the prevention of human-caused extinctions of rare invertebrate populations and their habitats. To a remarkable degree, insects and other invertebrates dominate animal life. Whether measured in terms of biomass or species, invertebrates make up 95 percent or more of animal life on earth. The Xerces Society is the only conservation group primarily dedicated to fostering invertebrates and invertebrate science in global conservation efforts. Because invertebrates sustain our biological systems, invertebrate conservation means preserving ecosystems and ecological functions as well as individual species.

Xerces Society publications include the magazine *Wings: Essays on Invertebrate Conservation* and the annual report of the Xerces North American Fourth of July Butterfly Count. Membership information is available from the Xerces Society headquarters, 10 Southwest Ash Street, Portland, Oregon 97204.

The Smithsonian Institution

is one of the world's leading research centers in the natural sciences with facilities located in the United States of America and the Republic of Panama. Consisting of fourteen museums and galleries—thirteen in Washington, D.C., and one in New York—as well as the National Zoological Park, the Smithsonian conducts research projects and educational programs in the arts, history, and sciences worldwide.

I offer this, then, as a formula of re-enchantment to reinforce poetry and myth: mysterious and little-known organisms still live within reach of where you sit. Splendor awaits in minute proportions.

E. O. WILSON,
XERCES SOCIETY PRESIDENT
AND BAIRD PROFESSOR OF SCIENCE,
HARVARD UNIVERSITY

Giant swallowtail (*Papilio cresphontes*) on lantana (*Lantana camara*). JOHN R. RIGGENBACH

CONTENTS

~

PREFACE

~

BY PUBLISHING *Butterfly Gardening: Creating Summer Magic in Your Garden*, the Xerces Society and the Smithsonian Institution hope to inspire you to include plants that attract butterflies in your garden. We want to arouse your interest in intricate, small-scale life systems so that you may come to appreciate the wonders of all insects. Your interest piqued, we hope you will take another step and add wildflowers indigenous to your area. Though the meadows and woodlands are nearly gone from our cities, planting native flora that attracts local butterflies serves as a reminder that we must protect and treasure our undisturbed natural areas.

Male fiery skipper (*Hylephila phyleus*) on statice (*Limonium* sp.). PETER J. BRYANT

Painted lady (*Vanessa cardui*) on daisy (*Chrysanthemum* sp.), Georgia.
JOHN R. RIGGENBACH

The impetus for a conservation-oriented book on butterfly gardening came from Spencer Beebe, vice president of Conservation International. Edwin Gould, curator of mammals at the National Zoological Park, launched *Butterfly Gardening: Creating Summer Magic in Your Garden*. Gould, a scientist as well as a gardener, initiated butterfly gardening on a grand scale at the National Zoological Park in 1984. In spring 1985, flower beds were planted with flowers that would lure the most butterflies, and the butterflies arrived, in surprising numbers and diversity. Zoo visitors were delighted.

The idea for a Xerces Society/Smithsonian Institution book on butterfly gardening emerged from a suggestion by Robert Robbins, assistant curator of Lepidoptera at the National Museum of Natural History, and a subsequent meeting with Gould. The Xerces Society and the Smithsonian Institution agreed to produce a book featuring spectacular photographs of butterflies and flowers, landscape designs, and essays by well-known lepidopterists and conservationists. Robbins; botanist Stanwyn G. Shetler, acting deputy director of the museum; and Xerces vice president Paul Opler provided the scientific information about butterflies and plants.

Butterfly Gardening: Creating Summer Magic in Your Garden is about designing and planting a butterfly garden. It also celebrates the diversity of butterflies. The book's overall aim is to promote broad-scale conservation of butterflies and their native food plants. The information and images emanate from the hearts and minds of Smithsonian and Xerces Society specialists who are concerned, committed conservationists. These individuals—scientists, photographers, writers, artists—are also gardeners who have spent countless sunny summer afternoons observing the multihued patterns and dancing grace of nature's four-winged lepidopteran fliers. They know, firsthand, that watching butterflies gives people a unique opportunity to observe the biological systems in their gardens at the level where, as E. O. Wilson puts it, "Splendor awaits in minute proportions."

Butterflies will come to our gardens and flourish if they find nectar and food plants there. Their presence will remind us of the essential bond we have with the natural world. Our hope is that scores of butterfly gardens will emerge in every city, suburb, and town—that gardeners will become directly engaged in the life cycle of butterflies and then in the biological systems of their gardens. By doing so, butterfly gardeners will find themselves guardians and curators of Lepidoptera—and, ultimately, stewards of nature.

Melody Mackey Allen,
EXECUTIVE DIRECTOR OF THE XERCES SOCIETY

Acknowledgments

THE PUBLICATION OF *Butterfly Gardening: Creating Summer Magic in Your Garden* was made possible through the combined efforts of writers, photographers, scientists, amateur lepidopterists, and gardeners. The Xerces Society is profoundly grateful to those who gave so generously of their talent and time.

While the names of authors and photographers appear alongside their work, other vital contributors to this project are less obvious to the reader. Funding from the Bingham Foundation made possible the initial planning of the book, solicitation and editing of articles, and collection of thousands of slides. Spencer Beebe, Dave Bohn, Wayne Booth, Ed Grosswiler, Paul Hawken, Kate Janeway, Howard Robinson, and Joe Spieler helped guide Xerces through its first foray into the world of book publishing; without their experience and counsel, this book would have never been published. Mary Troychak, Xerces Society publications editor, worked in concert with Xerces Society, Smithsonian Institution, and Sierra Club Books staff in developing the book from an outline to its present form. Editorial assistants Cheryl Bristah and Hollie Pietila and data manager Leif Pietila contributed crucial support. During the planning stages of the book, Xerces benefited from the expertise of the following people, who were critical in deciding the content and organization of the book: Joan DeWind, Christie Galen, Gail Gallagher, Bill Gilbert, Olivia Gilliam, Jeff Glassberg, Laine Johnson, Jeff Nekola, Roger Tory Peterson, Virginia Peterson, Judy Schneider, Philip Sheehan, and Craig Tufts. The following individuals read part or all of the manuscript at various stages and reviewed it for content and style: K. Eileen Allen, John Burns, Bill Carney, Frances Chew, Larry Gilbert, Ed Grosswiler, Fran Haselsteiner, Sue Hubbell, Wallace Huntington, Ed Knudson, John Laursen, Adair Law, Catherine Macdonald, Dennis D. Murphy, Paul A. Opler, Jerry A. Powell, Robert Michael Pyle, Robert K. Robbins, Iain Robertson, Art Shapiro, Stanwyn G. Shetler, Katrin B. Snow, Mathew Tekulsky, Kay Tomlinson, and Paul Wallulis.

Common sooty wing (*Philosora catullus*), Douglas County, Nebraska.
JOHN WEBER, JR.

We are also grateful to the lepidopterists, botanists, and gardeners who applied their expertise to the appendices: George Austin, Deane Bowers, Jo Brewer, F. Martin Brown, John V. Calhoun, Frances Chew, Jim Coleman, Charles V. Covell, Jr., Robert Dirig, Scott Ellis, Cliff Ferris, Greg Forbes, Larry Gilbert, L. Paul Grey, Jack Harry, Richard Heitzman, Ron Huber, Doris Jewett, Stan Jewett, Kurt Johnson, Ed Knudson, Robert Kral, Tim McCabe, Jeff Nekola, Mo Nielsen, Judy Pooler, Robert Michael Pyle, Robert K. Robbins, Dick Rosche, Ron Royer, Art Shapiro, Stephen Stone, Gayle Strickland, Richard Thoma, Mike Toliver, Craig Tufts, Wayne Wehling, Ralph Wells, and Dave Winter. The plant nomenclature was reviewed by John Kartesz, Biota of North America Program, University of North Carolina.

~

Male orange sulfur (*Colias eurytheme*) on red clover (*Trifolium pratense*).   JOHN R. RIGGENBACH

Introduction
~
Dennis D. Murphy

TUCKED AWAY IN THE family album is a photograph of a tow-headed kid clutching a Best Foods mayonnaise jar, an expression of wonder and joy on his face. Inside the jar is a sprig of milkweed and, clinging to it, a monarch butterfly. Jars and boxes of butterflies were to become commonplace for me from that time on—Dutchman's pipe with pipevine swallowtails, wild radish with cabbage butterflies, lawn grass with skippers. That nexus of caterpillars and host plants, the extraordinary process of metamorphosis, and the butterflies that emerged are among my clearest childhood memories.

Our garden, the fields behind it, and the creek across the road provided the setting for my first lessons in biological causes and effects. Recently I paid a visit to my old neighborhood only to find that the creek has been diverted; the grassy fields have given way to miles of housing, and the milkweeds are long since gone. Gone, too, are the old fences once entwined with passion vine—home and food for the spiny caterpillars that would become gulf fritillaries.

The gardens that captured the butterflies passing to and from their natural habitats in the fairly wild California that once surrounded us are now

Dennis D. Murphy is director of the Center for Conservation Biology at Stanford University. He is the author of more than ninety research articles and reviews on the population biology of butterflies and the conservation of rare and endangered species. He received a 1988 Chevron Conservation Award for his work in resolving conflicts between federal agencies and developers where endangered species are involved.

1

Monarch (*Danaus plexippus*), Santa Cruz, California.   FRANS LANTING

Female pipevine swallowtail (*Battus philenor*) on Joe-Pye-weed (*Eupatorium* sp.).
PETER W. POST

Larva of gulf fritillary (*Agraulis vanillae*) on passion vine (*Passiflora* sp.), Pima County, Arizona. STEVE PRCHAL, SONORAN ARTHROPOD STUDIES, INC.

almost bare. Butterflies just happened into gardens back then, but not anymore. Except for a few wide-ranging species with catholic tastes in larval host plants and sources of nectar, butterflies have become distant memories in most of suburban California. Lorquin's admiral, large marble, and silvery blue, once seemingly everywhere, have quietly vanished, along with the habitats that supported them, from the everyday world around us. Many of the butterflies that are now disappearing are not those generally recognized by law as endangered species. Endangered butterflies—such as the bay checkerspot, mission blue, and Lange's metalmark butterflies—never visited the average neighborhood garden. The loss of once-ubiquitous butterflies presents a new challenge to those concerned with butterfly conservation.

The disappearance of butterflies is an indicator of a greater loss, that of our native landscape and the species it supports. That loss of species diversity is but one of a multitude of environmental challenges we face—acid rain, polluted rivers and coastlines, widening holes in the ozone layer over polar regions, the build-up of "greenhouse" gases leading to global warming—all so grand in scale, so unmanageably complex in origin and resolution, that they seem to dwarf any attempts at conservation.

Despite the immensity of these global problems, conservation on a local level—through education and action—can go far to stem the assaults on our ecosystems. By protecting, restoring, and managing natural habitats in our own backyards, we can help protect those species with which we are familiar and whose disappearances we are already experiencing.

In the following articles, several active and well-known butterfly enthusiasts explore backyard conservation. From Great Britain, where biological diversity has suffered from man's sustained assault for centuries, Miriam Rothschild introduces us to her butterfly gardens and to the life history of the native large white butterfly that resides there. Dave Winter provides an overview of butterfly behavior and physiology, and Jo Brewer describes the relationship between host plants, butterflies, and the changing seasons. Melody Mackey Allen and Mary Booth provide the nuts and bolts of butterfly gardening—what to plant, how and where, for a balanced garden. Dave Winter reminds us to consider moths, the remaining 95 percent of the Lepidoptera that also benefit from butterfly gardens and that likewise contribute to the diversity of backyard plant–insect interactions. Stanwyn G. Shetler and David K. Northington place garden plants

Male gulf fritillary (*Agraulis vanillae*), Harris County, Texas.   GARY RETHERFORD

Female checkered white (*Pontia protodice*) taking nectar from shepherd's needle (*Bidens pilosa*). JOHN R. RIGGENBACH

and butterflies in their appropriate conservation context. Edward S. Ross, a true pioneer of close-up insect photography, shares his secrets of lens and flash in a how-to article on butterfly photography. Butterfly watcher and writer Robert Michael Pyle describes the incomparable experience of watching butterflies in their natural habitats.

The reintroduction of natural landscape elements into urban and suburban neighborhoods that are otherwise dominated by introduced species may be the greatest contribution to ecosystem conservation that we can make. Planting local native plant species in a rich, well-planned butterfly garden reduces the isolation of native plants in reserves and parks, provides essential corridors between remaining patches of habitat, and aids in repairing the patchwork of ecosystems that survive. "Plant a tree" is a popular exhortation to those who are concerned about our environment, but significantly more tangible value can be had from planting a garden, a small forest, or a diverse native plant community to support an assemblage of native butterflies. Such local conservation efforts provide not only much-needed havens for the creatures themselves, but they also offer a promise that future generations will have the opportunity to experience the delight of watching a butterfly flutter about on a fresh spring morning.

Male silver-studded blue (*Plebejus argus*). The blues were the first group to breed in the hay field.
KAZUO UNNO

Gardening with Butterflies
~
Miriam Rothschild

I GARDEN PURELY FOR pleasure. I love plants and flowers and green leaves, and I am incurably romantic, hankering after small stars spangling the grass. Butterflies add another dimension to the garden, for they are like dream flowers—childhood dreams—which have broken loose from their stalks and escaped into the sunshine. Air and angels. This is the way I look upon their presence, not as a professional entomologist, any more than I look upon roses as a botanist might, complaining that they are an impossibly difficult group.

I divide my garden into three rather distinct sections. First there is a conventional stone-walled kitchen garden with some half-derelict glasshouses in the middle. A variety of fruit trees—morello cherries, apricots, peaches, pears, greengages, and so forth—are grown along the inside of the wall. Plants are cultivated in rows, in trays, or in pots. The soil is a mixture of rich loams, some of it originally brought from the Bourne-

Miriam Rothschild is an eminent entomologist, an avid butterfly gardener, and a masterful writer on natural history. Her writing—a blend of scientific observations, literary quotations, and witty asides—has won her a following among scientists and lay people alike.

A member of a British banking family, Miriam Rothschild was educated at home. Her uncle Walter assembled a world-famous collection of two and a quarter million butterflies and moths; her father had thirty thousand specimens of fleas. Her chief interests have been parasitology and the relationship between animals and plants, although her work includes a much wider variety of subjects. She has also been involved in a wide range of causes and activities, including the rescue of refugees from Nazi Germany in the thirties and forties, the invention

Red admiral (*Vanessa atalanta*), a lover of ripe fruit in the walled garden, New Forest, England.   EDWARD S. ROSS

mouth area (heaven knows why!) by freight train around the turn of the century. I fancy that after eighty years in constant cultivation, with only an absolute minimum of sprays and insecticides, it harbors more than an average share of undesirable organisms. But that may be just an excuse when things go wrong—the 1980 epidemic of crown rot and red spider, for instance.

The second well-defined area is the house itself and the courtyard around which it is built. Here I have planted a wide variety of creepers and

of car seat belts, research into possible cures for schizophrenia, and better treatment of farm and laboratory animals. During the past ten years she has, almost singlehandedly, made Britain aware of its wildflower heritage and the threat posed to it by chemical spraying and fertilizing, highway construction, and urban expansion. At Ashton, her farm of several thousand acres in Peterborough, England, she has filled ninety acres of meadow with wildflowers and from there disseminated among the private and public gardens of her country the seeds of plants previously threatened with extinction or discarded as weeds. This article and the one that follows are reprinted from The Butterfly Gardener, *by Miriam Rothschild and Clive Farrell (London: Michael Joseph/Rainbird Publishing Group Limited, 1983).*

wall-trained shrubs for all seasons, ranging from Japanese quince and wis-teria to *Rosa banksiae*, bittersweet, bryonies, and varieties of clematis in-cluding traveller's joy or old man's beard. There is a fine profusion of gar-den flowers and wild species in a sort of grassy border where stone and soil meet around the foundations. A visitor arriving for the first time in this courtyard looked around at the untamed creepers and broom and the mauve and blue haze of candytuft and flax growing out of the gravel and, before ringing the bell, remarked uneasily, "I don't believe anyone can *live* here. . . ."

Finally, the third area consists of an acre of flowering hay field, divided from the house itself and its surrounding belt of flowers by a strip of closely cut lawn, a long bank of uncut grass and well-spaced-out wild cherry trees (by far my favorite tree), lilac bushes, a young ash or two with wild honeysuckle climbing up their branches, and a few crab apples, also growing in the long grass. The edges of a gravel path provide an additional mini-habitat.

Modern agricultural methods are unfortunately lethal both to wild-flowers and butterflies. Cowslips, buttercups, and blue and copper wings have been cultivated, drained, and bulldozed out of our fields. The smell of new-mown hay has been replaced by diesel fumes and clouds of dust;

European clouded yellow migrants (*Colias crocea*) passing through a hay field.
KAZUO UNNO

Lycaena phlaeas (small copper) caught in flight above mustard flowers.
KAZUO UNNO

while instead of haycocks, giant, circular, machine-made bales stand incongruously in the fields like the droppings of some mechanical monster. But with time and trouble and experimentation one can get wildflowers to grow in profusion in the grass or mixed in with the good old cultivated varieties. Thus we can entice a few butterflies back into our daily lives and hope they will dawdle and dally round the *Buddleia*. Wordsworth, in one of his most dreadful poems, had the same thought:

> *Stay near me—do not take thy flight,*
> *A little longer stay in sight.*
> *Much converse do I find in thee*
> *Historian of my infancy.*

But you can really abandon any romantic idea of creating a home for these angelic creatures—the best you can do is to provide them with a good pub. And like all popular wayside inns, it must have a plentiful supply of standard drinks always on tap.

One of the most common urban/suburban species in the American Northeast, the small copper is endangered in England.   KAZUO UNNO

Why do butterflies like some flowers more than others? Why is the taste and aroma of *Buddleia* nectar so infinitely more to their liking than the perfume and flavor of roses? We do not know. The fact is we know very little indeed about butterflies, but it is clear they prefer heavy perfume to delicate scents, and they must have the carbohydrates which they find in nectar, for flight demands a lot of energy.

This secretion is, broadly speaking, an aqueous solution of sugar, of which there are basically three types: one which contains sucrose (cane sugar), one fructose (fruit sugar, which is the sweetest of common sugars), and one glucose (corn or grape sugar). Sometimes all three sugars occur in the nectar of one species. The plants advertise the presence of this vital food source with a delicious variety of scent and color. The butterflies themselves exhale a delightful flowery fragrance. On a sunny day this mixture is like an umbrella of perfume spread across the garden, exciting the butterflies sexually, while the flowers are offering themselves freely in the interest of procreation.

Small tortoiseshell (*Nymphalis urticae*) lured to top-floor window by butterfly bush flowers (*Buddleia* sp.), Oxford, England.   EDWARD S. ROSS

It is worth noting that where taste and smell are concerned, butterflies are superior to us. They not only have chemical receptors on their tongues and antennae, but also on their feet. They can discriminate between the substance in Indian hemp which gives us a high and the cannabidiol which does not, whereas to the relatively feeble human nose these two are indistinguishable.

Abraham Cowley in "The Wish" says: "May I a small house and a large garden have," and this I believe is the right approach. Even with a dearth of hands, which leads inescapably to a wilderness, I doubt a garden can ever be too large, certainly not from the butterfly's viewpoint. But so many of us are forced to be satisfied with a small patch of ground that it is an agreeable thought that butterflies can be attracted to tiny gardens as well as large ones. A *Buddleia* planted against your house, a patch of red valerian growing out of a wall, or a lavender bush constitutes a true butterfly lure.

Like Alfred, Lord Tennyson, I favor "a careless order'd garden," though growing wildflowers is no easier than cultivating the conventional, well-tried horticultural varieties. In some ways it is more difficult, because not much is known about them. I doubt if you can easily find a book that tells you how to grow the lesser celandine or selfheal in a garden, or how to keep order in a little wilderness. Nor for that matter are wildflowers essential as butterfly lures, but they are a great help. Moreover, growing wild species not only preserves them from extinction (for who can doubt that cowslips will one day be as rare as the lady's slipper orchid, thanks to our sprays and combines and ditching equipment), but also provides special nectar sources for butterflies.

A new type of municipal horticulture is just around the corner, in which the parks in new towns and the road verges and roundabouts will be sown with a flowering meadow mixture instead of a dreary mono-crop of coarse grass. The rise in the price of fuel has done us one good turn: it

White peacock (*Anartia jatrophae*) on lantana (*Lantana camara*).
JOHN R. RIGGENBACH

Red admiral (*Vanessa atalanta*) on pickerel-weed (*Pontederia cordata*).
JOHN R. RIGGENBACH

has reduced the needless cutting of road verges, and in many areas wild-flowers are already enhancing our dreary motorways. This roadside flora turns the verges into butterfly highways, a link between woods and nature reserves, which have rapidly become like a series of oases in a desert of sprayed and smoking corn fields. Road cuttings with steep banks are ideal sunny spots for wildflowers and butterflies. If you have a bank in your garden, cherish it.

About two hundred years ago, Joseph Addison remarked in the *Spectator* that he valued his garden "for being fuller of blackbirds than of cherries." I agree with him, although there are times when you sigh and wish it were otherwise. Last summer I watched with mixed feelings a charm of goldfinches descend on a row of goatsbeard and pick the plants to pieces and rob the seeds before the "clocks" developed. I was saving them all carefully for sowing. But no one in their senses would exchange goldfinches for a row of goatsbeard, however fascinating their huge clocks may be. I encourage all the birds, although bullfinches (which demolish cherry and apple blossoms, presumably looking for insects or even nectar) are beautiful but pestilential and destructive creatures. And I have a passion for robins singing in the rain. I believe their songs to be outbursts of beautiful rage. I willingly sacrifice the odd butterfly for their sake.

In a small garden you are much more conscious of insect pests, snails, and field voles than you are in a large one. You know each plant individually, and it gets under your skin if you see your roses covered in greenfly, or the tender leaves chewed up by remorseless slugs, or half-opened cherry blossoms littering the path, or foliage scalloped by leaf-cutting bees. But if you really want butterflies in the garden, you have to reduce sprays to an absolute minimum and abstain from slug pellets.

In my own garden, in the open, I have used no insecticides or weed killers or seed dressings for the last ten years, but I have sprayed diligently against fungi and greenfly, in the latter case with a simple detergent, Lux. And I bring in all the ladybirds I can find—especially in the larval stage—and put them on the roses, hoping they will help to check the greenfly. Ladybirds, however, like butterflies, are apt to move on. Undoubtedly the birds destroy a lot of insects, both good and bad, and in the process take their toll of flower buds and seeds. The butterflies in their turn pollinate many of my flowers, though their young stages chew up the cabbages and nasturtium leaves. But by and large I give nature a free hand, and I am rewarded by the pair of nightingales singing close to the house and, at the moment of writing, by thirteen species of butterflies on the wing and over a hundred species of wildflowers and grasses in the garden.

Male purplish copper (*Lycaena helloides*). JOHN WEBER, JR.

What Do Butterflies See?

Miriam Rothschild

IT APPEARS HIGHLY probable that butterflies, as we do, "seem naturally attracted to give special attention to all colored substances."

In the garden we should plan to please the small copper and the blues as well as ourselves. But what do butterflies see?

It is not possible to describe the color red to a person blind from birth. It is almost as difficult to try to imagine what the sky looks like to a butterfly, because, unlike you or me, it can see polarized light—the light waves vibrating at right angles to the direction in which they are traveling. If we were standing at the bottom of a deep well at midday with only a small patch of blue sky visible, we might look upward and see the odd star shining, but we could not tell the direction of the sun. A butterfly could do so, for the rays of polarized light indicate the sun's position, like a sort of sun compass. But what does it all *look* like? Does the sky seem slatted to a butterfly—alternate lines of bright light and shade, like a Venetian blind or the old Japanese flag—or does the sky seem darker blue-green away from the sun, or is the vault of heaven dismembered into sectors that differ in color or intensity? Does this pattern shift relative to the butterfly as its line of vision or its direction of flight changes? Should we think of it as another unimaginable sort of color vision? Like many other things, we simply do not know.

Some aspects of insect eyes and insect vision can be tested by observation and experiment. We know, for instance, that butterflies' eyes, which bulge outward from their heads, are composed of thousands of separate

17

Butterflies' eyes are composed of hundreds of separate lenses set closely together and so arranged that the butterfly can see all around itself—not just forward—without turning its head. Female orange sulfur (*Colias eurytheme*) on composite, Antioch, California.   EDWARD S. ROSS

lenses (ommatidia) set closely together and so arranged that the butterfly can see all around itself—not just forward—without turning its head. The butterfly's world must seem like a well-lit bowl. Also, the lenses in the bottom half of many insects' eyes are different from the rest—specialized for close-up vision. In fact, they provide natural bifocals. In certain species, these bifocals only see color in the bottom half; the top sees the world as a black-and-white film.

Butterflies can see more colors than we do. Perhaps their appreciation of the red end of the spectrum is not as good as ours, but unlike us, at the opposite end they can see into the ultraviolet. (In fact, it is with their ultraviolet receptors that they can appreciate polarized light.) Many flowers that seem uniformly colored to us, like the glossy yellow lesser celandine, if photographed under an ultraviolet light, reveal dark nectar guides around the center. These petal guidelines—invisible to us—assist a flying insect in finding the spot where the nectar is stored, suggesting they tend

Unlike humans, butterflies can see into the ultraviolet end of the spectrum. This sunflower (*Helianthus annuus*) was photographed under normal light and then under ultraviolet light to illustrate what a butterfly might see.
GARY RETHERFORD

Male Eastern tailed blue (*Everes comyntas*), Great Smokies, North Carolina.
EDWARD S. ROSS

to be nearsighted. Flowers pollinated by hummingbirds, which have marvelously acute far sight, are not provided with nectar guides. Many male butterflies signal to their females with the aid of ultraviolet, which, as they flap their wings, glances off their specially structured scales like tiny flashes of lightning.

Some tropical butterflies and moths have transparent wings. These insects probably can signal by means of polarized light, for the scaleless wing veins glow like molten gold if they are viewed under a microscope with the appropriate polarizing filters.

Some biologists believe that moths can sense the individual infrared patterns emitted by plants in the dark. We are conscious of the infrared reflection in photographs of bluebell woods because the beautiful azure tint is lost, and because of the sensitivity of the photographic emulsion on the film to infrared, they appear a rather disappointing mauve. Butterflies probably see these flowers as a brighter blue color than we do, since they are less sensitive to the longer waves of light. For this reason, you would expect poppies to be less exciting to insects than they are to us; but apart from their red color they reflect ultraviolet, and the effect must be greatly accentuated by the crinkled petals, so that, presumably, they shine and flash as they shake in the breeze. A number of species, however, do not see red at all, and to them the beautiful scarlet poppies would look black with a silver glance. This may account for the fact that very often the fresh young shoots and leaves of plants are colored red instead of green. The butterflies thus overlook them when laying eggs, and the tender new growth is spared destruction by voracious caterpillars.

None will deny that color rather than shape attracts the ordinary gardener to flowers. The rose 'Etoile de Hollande' may be perfectly shaped, but it would lose much of its attraction if it were the same shade as the leaves. Butterflies, like us, rate color above outline. From a distance the flower border is a blur of lovely shades and subtle tones and brilliant patches of colored light. We both fail to distinguish individual shapes and sizes, but the distant view of flowers has a special attraction, like the *Fata Morgana*. Once a chance visitor to my bluebell wood, on catching sight of this wonderful azure sea, stripped naked and plunged in among the flowers. This struck a casual passerby as extraordinarily eccentric. But was it? The passing small tortoiseshell butterfly may also be overcome by the blue perfumed air and sink in ecstasy among the serried ranks of ultramarine bells.

To appeal to a butterfly's eye, stands of flowers are better than single ones, and the finest combination is yellow and mauve with a sweet scent. Robert Bridges thought that if odor were visible as color, he would see the summer garden aureoled in rainbow clouds. It is easy to imagine that the butterflies on a summer afternoon are caught up in a golden bowl of light in which scent and color are inextricably mixed.

Little metalmarks (*Calephelis virginiensis*) mating on Queen Anne's lace (*Daucus carota*).
JOHN R. RIGGENBACH

The Struggle to Survive

Dave Winter

T HE WONDER OF LEPIDOPTERA—butterflies and moths—lies not just in their beauty. Considering the adverse odds they face, it is a wonder they are here at all.

In developing from egg to free-flying adult, Lepidoptera pass through four life stages. There are specific environmental requirements for each species at its various stages, and there are potential hazards for individuals at each stage. An appreciation of these stages, environmental needs, and hazards can increase both the enjoyment and effectiveness of gardening for butterflies.

The four life stages through which Lepidoptera pass—egg, larva, pupa, and adult—constitute "complete metamorphosis": there is virtually no similarity in appearance between the forms of the immature stages and that of the adult. The egg, with its tough shell to protect the developing embryo within, varies in size from a fraction of a millimeter in the smallest moths and butterflies to more than two millimeters in the largest moths. It may be round or shaped like a spindle, a turban, a hemisphere, or a pancake; and its surface may appear as smooth as a billiard ball or as intricately sculptured as a finely carved chalice. The color of the shell may change as the egg develops, and in some species the larva's dark head may be seen

Dave Winter *is secretary of the Lepidopterists' Society. He is a former editor of the society's* NEWS *and chaired the society's collecting guidelines committee. He is coauthor, with his wife, Jo Brewer, of* Butterflies and Moths: A Companion to Your Field Guide *(Englewood Cliffs, N.J.: Prentice-Hall, 1986).*

Chalcedon checkerspots (*Euphydryas chalcedona*) mating (male on left), Mill Valley, California.   EDWARD S. ROSS

Chalcedon checkerspot (*Euphydryas chalcedona*) laying eggs on sticky monkey flower (*Mimulus aurantiacus*), Mill Valley, California.   EDWARD S. ROSS

Full-grown larva of chalcedon checkerspot (*Euphydryas chalcedona*), Mill Valley, California.

EDWARD S. ROSS

Prepupal larva of chalcedon checkerspot (*Euphydryas chalcedona*), Mill Valley, California.

EDWARD S. ROSS

Chrysalid of chalcedon checkerspot (*Euphydryas chalcedona*), Mill Valley, California.

EDWARD S. ROSS

Female chalcedon checkerspot (*Euphydryas chalcedona*) warming flight muscles by basking in the sun, Mill Valley, California. EDWARD S. ROSS

Some species lay eggs singly: egg of gulf fritillary (*Agraulis vanillae*) on passion vine leaf (*Passiflora* sp.), Texas.   GARY RETHERFORD

moving about inside on the last day of development. The larva frees itself by chewing a hole through the eggshell; in many instances it then consumes most or all of the shell. At the time of hatching the larva looks three times too large ever to have been enclosed within the shell. If it is to bear horns or spines, these pop up like little periscopes within the first few minutes of freedom.

The larva has three main parts: head, thorax, and abdomen. In nearly all lepidopterous larvae, the head has six pairs of tiny, single eyes (rather than the elaborate compound eyes of the adult), a pair of mandibles which bite together from the sides, and silk glands, with which it builds its various structures and lifelines. In most larvae, the thorax is made up of three segments and bears three pairs of true legs; these are eventually modified (in the pupa) to become the legs of the adult moth or butterfly. The pads which will later give rise to wings are inverted within the thorax and are not visible on the larva. Most of the larva's body is abdomen, made up of ten segments, occupied largely by the digestive tract.

A larva is an eating machine. Watch a tomato hornworm in the garden sometime. With the leaf edge stabilized between its feet, the larva moves its head in rhythmic downward arcs, the mandibles chomping off chunk after chunk of the leaf. The leaf disappears at a prodigious rate.

A larva grows in a series of stages, or instars. Periodically (four times in the usual five instars) the larva stops eating for a while. It has grown a new and larger head capsule under the skin behind the old one, and a new skin within the old. It then pops off the old head capsule, crawls out of the old skin, and resumes eating. The rigid head capsule cannot grow in size, but the skin does stretch significantly during each instar. Under favorable, warm temperature conditions, a larva may complete its feeding in three to six weeks.

At the end of the last larval instar, the larva stops eating and searches for a while for a place to pupate. Then an organism of totally different form develops. In most cases, it has no external appendages except some tiny hooks at the tip of the abdomen. The pupa remains quiescent, except for an occasional twitch or wriggle if it is disturbed. And within it the structures of the larva are being broken down and rebuilt into the structures necessary for the adult butterfly or moth to perform its tasks.

Pupal life span is temperature-related; often there are long delays. After seven to fourteen days of pupal development, the color pattern of the maturing moth or butterfly may become visible through the wing cases of the pupal shell. The adult insect is about to emerge. It bursts open the pupa, clambers out, and promptly climbs to a sheltered spot where its miniature, soft, crumpled wings can hang down and expand.

The wing of a moth or butterfly is composed of a transparent, tough membrane supported by hollow, riblike veins. When the adult emerges from the pupa, these structures are soft, shrunken, and floppy. As the insect pumps fluid into the veins, they elongate, fan out, and harden to form an orderly, rigid, supporting framework with the membrane lying smoothly between them. Expansion and hardening time can vary from ten to twenty minutes in the smallest species to several hours in the largest moths.

Lepidoptera. The name is of Greek origin, meaning "scale-winged." In most species the wing membrane itself is not visible, because it is densely shingled on each surface with tiny scales which form the distinctive colors and patterns of each species. The scales, which may be likened to minute canoe paddles, are attached to the wing by their "handles." Each scale has its particular color, some from pigment and some from the diffraction of light on an intricately ridged and grooved surface. This effect, which works like a prism, is called structural coloration.

Does a butterfly die if the scales are rubbed off its wings? It does not, but when butterflies lose many of their wing scales, their thermoregulatory and courtship functions are lost, and their flying efficiency is reduced.

Like the larva, the adult butterfly is organized into head, thorax, and abdomen, but what a difference! The eyes are large and semispherical, a

Undersurface of hindwing, black swallowtail (*Papilio polyxenes*). The shingled arrangement of the scales is apparent in the orange patches. The metallic blue dots are single scales; diffraction produces their color.   ALAN K. CHARNLEY

honeycomb arrangement of hundreds of separate facets which detect movement, pattern, and color. Their color vision extends well into the ultraviolet portion of the spectrum, far beyond the range of human vision. From between the eyes protrude two antennae equipped with chemical receptors for smell and with pressure receptors that detect variations in wind speed as well as direction to aid the insect in controlling its flight path.

Their antennae distinguish butterflies from moths. A butterfly's antenna ends in a small knob or club (or, in the case of skippers, a small hook). Moths have antennae which are plumelike, feathery, or threadlike. A few minor exceptions exist, but in such cases other features of the insect clarify whether it is a butterfly or a moth.

The adults of most Lepidoptera have a long proboscis, bipartite and laid out straight as it emerges from the pupa. The two halves of the tongue are etched with longitudinal ridges and grooves that work like a Ziploc® closure. While its wings are expanding and hardening, the insect fits the tongue's two sides together to form a hollow sipping straw, which it then coils neatly beneath its head. The silk glands are lost in the process of metamorphosis.

In addition to the wings, the thorax bears three pairs of legs equipped with pads and claws (tarsi) for climbing and clinging and with chemical sensors to aid in food-plant selection. In a few families of butterflies the first pair of legs is reduced in size, sometimes to the point where they serve only sensory functions.

The abdomen is relatively smaller than that of the larva, but it has the same ten segments. The principal contents of the abdomen are the reproductive organs and stored energy reserves, which are mainly in the form of fat. Excretory and circulatory functions also occur there.

Once the moth or butterfly has put its proboscis in order and its wings are expanded and stiff, it gets on with the important tasks of the adult stage: feeding, mating, and, in the case of females, egg laying. Adults of the large silkmoths, such as the luna and the cecropia, have no functioning mouth parts or digestive system. They do not feed. They subsist entirely on their own stored fat, left over from the larval stage. Other species of butterflies and moths alternate episodes of feeding with mate-finding activities. Food sources are usually floral nectar, sap runs at a broken twig or branch, decomposing fruit, or juices from carrion and feces.

With scores of species of butterflies or moths on the wing at any given time and place, an efficient means of locating a mate of the correct species is critical, and the strategies for doing this are many. The tiger swallowtail will patrol a "beat" along forest paths or about a meadow in search of a female. If you wait and watch, you may see the same butterfly go by the same spot from the same direction every five minutes or so. Others, such as the dusky wing skipper, will perch on an isolated twig or weed stalk and dash out to investigate any dark flying object remotely resembling itself in size. If the passing insect is a male dusky wing, a "dogfight" ensues, with the two spiraling rapidly up and out of sight. If a female is engaged, mating may follow. Other species practice "hilltopping": males patrol about the tops of small hills, waiting for a female to come by.

A butterfly's ability to recognize objects at a distance is visual and rather imprecise. Every male cloudless sulfur that happens by a piece of yellow paper attached to a stick will investigate. Where fritillaries are flying, a male will veer toward an orange tossed into the air before it falls to the ground. At closer range, the butterfly's eyesight allows it to recognize specific details of pattern. In some species of sulfurs and whites, flashing reflections of ultraviolet light, invisible to humans, enable the butterfly to distinguish sex and species.

The most finely tuned recognition is often through specific chemical scents called pheromones, which confirm identification and also encourage receptiveness on the part of the female. These pheromones are disseminated by brushlike hairs on the wings or legs of males or the abdomens of both males and females.

Many moths, operating in darkness with reduced opportunities for visual recognition, rely on pheromones emitted from glands at the end of the female's abdomen. In larger moths, such as silkmoths, the pheromone is so potent that it can draw males upwind from as far as several miles away. A single molecule is sufficient to trigger a response in a sensor cell on the male's antenna. A "calling" female silkmoth, set out in a cage, is often surrounded by dozens or even hundreds of ardent males within just a few minutes.

In most moths, chemical differences in the pheromones is the key to interspecific recognition. Because numerous pheromones from different species can be floating about on the breezes at the same time, some remarkable adaptations have evolved to reduce confusion among closely related moths. In the southeastern United States, three species of *Callosamia* silkmoths fly during the same season. The promethea female calls and the males fly in late afternoon, starting about 4 P.M. The tulip tree silkmoth calls for a few hours starting about 10 P.M., and the sweetbay silkmoth starts calling about 10 A.M., stopping about an hour before the promethea's calling time. While promethea and sweetbay males are strictly day fliers, the females of all three species fly and lay eggs only at night.

Once mating has begun, Lepidoptera remain paired for periods of many minutes to many hours, depending on size of insect, time of day, the weather, and, most important, whether the male mated previously. Following separation the male goes back to his feeding and mate-seeking activities. The female may rest until her normal flying time or do some feeding, but she soon gets down to the business of egg laying.

In contrast to birds, Lepidoptera take no responsibility for their offspring once the eggs are laid. But since most species are strictly limited to one or more species of host plant on which their larvae can survive and thrive, the female must be able to locate the proper plants. The black swallowtail slowly fluttering near the carrot leaves in the garden will land, test them with her feet, then pause and curl her abdomen down, gluing an egg to the leaf surface. The leaves of tansy and yarrow, which are somewhat similar to those of carrots, may be given passing attention, but they are quickly rejected as unpalatable for the larvae. The American painted lady will alight on a leaf of pearly everlasting, tap-tap-tap with her feet, and then move forward to tuck an egg into the leaf fuzz at exactly the spot where she was tapping. Many species insert eggs in plant tissue or lay their eggs loosely.

Eggs are almost always attached to the plant with quick-drying glue. There may be a single egg, a few in one place, or a batch of hundreds in one patch. In some of the batch-laying species, such as the American tent caterpillar, the larvae remain together, feeding in large aggregations, at least in the early instars. In others, like the gypsy moth, they quickly disperse upon hatching. If the egg is destined to remain unhatched through the winter, it will usually be placed on the bark or leaves of the host plant. A few species place the egg on the ground near the host plant, and some species of the rather primitive ghost moths merely fly over an area where the host plant grows, broadcasting thousands of minute eggs haphazardly over the ground.

Larval host plants can vary with geography and season. The luna moth in northern New England usually eats beech and yellow birch, but farther south, where hickories and black walnut grow, those are the preferred host plants.

The larvae of a few species of Lepidoptera are carnivorous. Those of the harvester butterfly devour woolly aphids as their only food. Ants carry the larvae of some of the small blue butterflies into their nests, and there the butterfly larvae proceed to dine on ant larvae. *Cosmia calami*, a noctuid moth, begins its larval feeding on oak leaves, but as the larvae become more robust they switch to other larvae.

When the larva is full grown it stops eating and empties out the contents of its gut, leaving a small, dark puddle. In many species the larva then searches for a safe spot in which to pupate. This may be a move of a few inches to an adjacent leaf or stem or a trek of hundreds of feet to locate soft soil in which the larva can bury itself. Some larvae do not wander at all: they pupate within the homemade leaf shelter where they have hidden throughout their growing days.

In most butterflies the pupa is called a chrysalid (derived from the Greek word for gold), because in some species it is decorated with gold or silver markings. In the families Nymphalidae and Satyridae it is suspended upside-down from a silk pad, into which hooks at the end of the abdomen are thrust. Most swallowtails and sulfurs are additionally supported by a silk girdle or "seat belt" which the prepupal larva spins. The contortions the larva goes through as it constructs this seat belt are a fascinating sight.

Some moth larvae construct cocoons, carefully created silken bags within which pupation occurs. Most moths are not adapted to move forward within or from the cocoon; the pupae remain in situ for emergence. But many moth pupae are naked and are formed within leaf litter on the ground or in the soil, the larva having tunneled several inches below the surface. How, in that case, does the moth escape at emergence time? Some pupae have rings of backward-pointing spines at the edges of their abdominal segments. As the pupa alternately telescopes and extends its abdomen, the spines catch against the soil and thrust the pupa upward to the surface.

The most frequently heard question is How long does a butterfly (or moth) live? The answers are varied. A butterfly's expected life span takes into consideration physiological limits as well as field averages, including predation losses. For example, the black swallowtail has a maximum time in the field of thirty-five to forty days but an average of ten to twelve days. Many small blues and coppers live only a few days. The great silkmoths, which are unable to feed as adults, weaken and die after about a week. In a species that is breeding continuously and producing several generations in the course of a summer, such as the cabbage white butterfly, the adult life span may be one to five weeks. Captive underwing moth females, fed daily, have continued to lay eggs for over a month. The female zebra butterfly of southern Florida is able to thrive and lay eggs for as long as six months. Monarchs, mourning cloaks, and many moths are adults for six to ten months, although inactive much of that time.

But this is only part of the story, and it leads to the subject of diapause.

Diapause, with emphasis on the "pause," is a period of more or less suspended development in the life cycles of Lepidoptera. It serves to tide individuals over a period when food is unavailable or when the climate is inimical to continued growth and development or to reproductive activities. In temperate climates this period covers the colder months of the year, and in tropical climates it is more common during the dry season, when vegetation is tough and dry and nectar-producing flowers are scarce. The adult butterflies that hibernate, such as the anglewing butterflies, live from late summer to April or May, but the adults of the summer generation, offspring of these hibernators, may live only two or three weeks. Some fall-emerging moths have a winter diapause and lay eggs in the spring. Their larvae mature rapidly on the lush spring foliage, pupate, and then experience diapause again, as pupae, through the heat of summer.

Just when hibernation occurs varies with the group. In some species, the larvae feed in the fall, pupate in a sheltered spot, and await the return of warm weather before completing their development. Dusky wing skippers winter over as fully fed larvae, pupating in the spring and emerging shortly thereafter. Checkerspot butterflies and many inchworms hibernate when only partially grown. The viceroy and its relatives do likewise, each larva constructing its own garagelike hibernaculum, tailored to precisely its own size and secured by silk to the twig on which it hangs exposed all winter. Fritillary larvae hatch from their eggs in the fall. They then hibernate immediately in the leaf litter without feeding, waiting for the young violet leaves to unfold in spring.

Many species of moths and butterflies go through diapause in the egg stage. Some underwing eggs hatch at the time of bud burst in the spring and the larvae feed rapidly on the new, tender foliage, before tannins and other compounds accumulate to make the leaves tougher and less palatable. The adults then produce eggs in which diapause lasts from summer to the following spring.

Multiple periods of diapause can occur within one generation. In higher latitudes larvae from summer eggs hatch, feed for a while, and then hibernate through the long, cold winter; the second summer they feed and hibernate again; the third summer they finish feeding, pupate, and promptly emerge as adults. If generations do not overlap, then that species of butterfly emerges and flies only in alternate years. In one scenario, the carpenterworm larva makes such slow progress boring and eating its way through the trunks of living hardwood trees that it has to hibernate through two winters before maturing in its third summer.

Prolonged diapause is another phenomenon which extends life spans in some species. In ecosystems stabilized by periodic natural fires, species like the buck moth protect their offspring with an effective form of insurance. A considerable percentage of a summer's pupae will not produce adults the same autumn; adult emergence is delayed until the autumn one or even several years later. If a fire during the larval feeding season happens to destroy a particular generation, the "holdover" pupae from the previous generation can sustain the population. Because the pupae are buried beneath the surface of the ground, a quickly passing fire does not harm them.

The longest prolonged diapause is not yet known. In 1969 Jerry Powell, a California lepidopterist, collected yucca plants harboring a large number of yucca moth larvae. Prepupal larvae produced several hundred adults during the sixteenth to twentieth seasons. Fifteen percent of the larvae emerged in 1989, twenty years later. More prepupal larvae remain alive. So the question How long does a moth live? has, as yet, no absolute answer.

There is much to be learned about the movement of butterflies. Does a butterfly live out its life span close to where it emerged from its chrysalid? Or does it move to adjacent areas where the nectaring or mate-finding opportunities may be greater, the larval host plant in greater numbers or better condition, or the numbers of its own species lower and the competition less? This subject has been studied in detail for a few species, and various patterns have been defined.

Some species will indeed remain largely within a specialized habitat, such as a bog, particularly if other areas with acceptable habitat are widely scattered. Other species, adapted to a more broadly available habitat, may seek mates or lay eggs in an area one day and move a mile or so on the next day, so that there may be a continual flow of individuals from one place to another. Thus, the butterfly nectaring in your garden today may just be passing through and not be "your own" butterfly. Noticing details of wing damage can help you recognize a specific individual from day to day. Capturing a butterfly, marking the underside of a wing with a felt-tip pen, and releasing it also helps you recognize an individual on successive sightings.

A butterfly's ability to move is not automatic. Lepidoptera are "cold-blooded"—at rest their body temperatures are close to that of the surrounding environment. The internal temperature of the wing muscles within the thorax must usually be about 75°–110° F for vigorous flight; and on a spring or fall day or in the cool of the morning, a butterfly may have to raise its internal temperature fifteen to twenty degrees in order to fly. While a few species partially raise their temperature by shivering (rapidly contracting their flight muscles so the wings vibrate but do not flap), most do so by basking—exposing the thorax, abdomen, and bases of their wings to the sun's heat. The butterfly resting in the sun with its wings spread flat against a dark patch of ground is soaking up heat both from the sun's rays above and from the dark earth beneath. Within a minute or two its body temperature can reach flight level, and thereafter the combination of the sun's heat and internal heat production suffice to maintain flight. Yet if a cloud obscures the sun, airflow overcools the body and the butterfly settles to the ground to await another opportunity to warm itself. The sulfur butterflies bask differently. They fold their wings over their back and tip over sideways so that the sun's rays strike them at a perpendicular angle. Butterflies which rely upon basking have dark bodies and dark scaling at their wing bases so they absorb more heat.

Control of overheating is equally important, since sustained or repeated high temperatures (above 113° F) can shorten life span and reduce egg production. Many butterflies seek shade and reduce activity at air temperatures of 100° F to 110° F. Some species refrain from flying in open sunlight during the heat of the day. Others stand on "tip-toes" on the ground, wings folded over the back and oriented so that they cast no shadow.

Most moths, unable to warm themselves in the sun, utilize shivering. The heavy-bodied sphinx moths and the great silkmoths vibrate their wings intensely for a minute or two before zooming or flapping. Yet many microlepidoptera, the size of the clothes moth, seem to have muscles adapted to low-temperature operation: when threatened, they can take off instantly at temperatures only ten degrees above freezing.

Most eggs Lepidoptera lay will never become moths or butterflies. Although each female moth or butterfly can lay hundreds of eggs, if an average of two offspring from each mating pair survive to become successfully reproductive adults, the population of that species will remain stable from year to year. If all larvae were to survive (as can happen if they are reared carefully in captivity), we would probably not be here to write or read this book. What natural forces limit population growth?

Hazards are present at every stage of lepidopteran development. Beetles and birds consume large numbers of eggs—they are among the quarry that the brown creeper is seeking as it works over a tree trunk. Parasitoids (organisms whose development within another species results in the death of the host) destroy many. Sometimes, for example, a swallowtail or sphinx moth egg has a mottled rather than a uniformly pearly look, evidence that inside are developing several *dozen* wasps, so small that they are barely visible to the unaided eye.

Parasitoid chalcid wasps on chrysalid of gulf fritillary (*Agraulis vanillae*), Pena Blanca, Arizona.   EDWARD S. ROSS

The larva has even more with which to cope. Most songbirds rear their young on the larvae of Lepidoptera and other insects. It is no accident that birds nest when the largest number of larvae is growing the fastest. Hornets, wasps, bugs, and spiders also take their share, either sucking the larvae dry or chopping them up into pieces of transportable size. Parasitoids—at this stage tachinid flies and ichneumonid, chalcid, and braconid wasps—destroy large numbers. Some parasitoids emerge from the larval stage, some from the pupa. It is a rare tomato hornworm that does not end up dangling and limp, a cluster of white braconid pupae attached to its skin.

As if these risks were not enough, the larvae also have to contend with bacterial and viral diseases, which can suddenly terminate the outbreak of a pest species, such as the gypsy moth. The commercially available *Bacillus thuringensis* (BT), a bacterium, is effectively used as a larvicide. Unfortunately, its effects are not limited to the pest species to which it may be applied, so it can be deleterious to other lepidopteran species.

Mortality among pupae, other than that caused by the emergence of parasitoid wasps, is probably the work of birds and mammals. Mortality at all stages is, of course, abetted by humans, not only through the use of pesticides, but also through the human penchant for neatness. In gardens, no doubt countless larvae and pupae, which had chosen shelter of presumed secrecy and safety among the leaf litter, are gathered up and composted all in the name of order. Natural debris is a necessity for many Lepidoptera.

The moth or butterfly emerges from the pupa, successfully expands its wings, and embarks on a career of reproduction. Is the battle won? Not at all. Predators, both vertebrate and arthropod, are the next obstacle to overcome. Songbirds and lizards successfully catch and eat butterflies; bats hunt moths at night. Hornets pounce on roosting Lepidoptera. Assassin bugs, ambush bugs, dragonflies, and flower spiders all take their toll, capturing the insects as they alight on flowers to take nectar. A praying mantis will lurk about, capturing even the largest butterflies.

With such a litany of doom, can moths and butterflies do anything to defend themselves? They can do a great deal, and their protective strategies are among the most fascinating features of Lepidoptera.

Egg protection is rather straightforward: they are hidden, whether in chinks in bark or on the undersurface of a leaf. A thatch of irritating hairs from the abdomen of the female may cover a mass of eggs. But some females, such as the viceroy and question mark, often place the egg on the tip of a leaf.

Larvae excel in dissembling. They can have the color and pattern of the leaf on which they feed or of the stem on which they rest. They can

The remains of a monarch (*Danaus plexippus*) which blundered into the web of an orb-weaving spider (*Argiope aurantia*), Chiles Valley, California.
EDWARD S. ROSS

bear diagonal lines which, against a background of mixed vegetation, obscure their cylindrical shape. They can look like bits of curled or dying leaf or can rest motionless, at an angle from a twig, looking exactly like another twig, complete with bark and end buds. They can rest in groups, looking like the skeletonized end of a partly eaten leaf. Some are highly accurate replicas of bird droppings. Some flower feeders change to the color of the flower on which they are feeding, and some decorate their backs with ragged bits nipped from the host flower. Color, pattern, and even overall shape can change strikingly from one instar to the next, usually in conjunction with a change in behavior dictated by the larva's increasing size. But each instar has one major characteristic in common with the others: it makes the larva look less like a "worm" and more like something either invisible or inedible. It is not clear how effectively these tactics mislead birds, but they certainly mislead humans!

Larvae sometimes use protective behaviors. Some will drop from the host plant when disturbed and lie motionless in the leaf litter, climbing back later to resume feeding. A larva approached by a parasitoid fly or wasp will often whip the front half of its body back and forth violently in a frequently successful effort to drive the creature away. The presence of a par-

Male cloudless sulfur (*Phoebis sennae*), victim of a spider, on a composite. JOHN R. RIGGENBACH

asitoid among some communally feeding butterfly larvae will set up a synchronized twitching within the group that deters the intruder.

The hairs, horns, or spines which some larvae bear may be defensive in nature. The branching spines on many butterfly larvae are innocuous to humans but may make them unpalatable to birds. The fine hairs of the gypsy moth larva are irritating to the stomachs of most birds; only cuckoos eat them with impunity. Some moth larvae, such as those of the io and the buck moths, have spines which sting more intensely than nettles. Yet the fiercest-looking of all, the hickory horn devil, has inchlong "antlers" that are a complete sham.

The larvae of some blues work a "deal" with certain species of ants. Glands on the abdomen produce a sweet secretion which the ants consume. In return, the ants protect the larvae by swarming all over the threatening parasitoids and arthropod predators.

Swallowtail larvae, such as the spicebush swallowtail, have a combination of features which give them a snakelike appearance. The forepart of the body is swollen and displays an eyelike spot on each side; the creature rests in a rolled leaf shelter with only its front end visible. When disturbed it thrusts out a forked, orange structure (the osmeterium), resembling a snake's tongue and emitting a sweetish but disagreeable odor. Although it has never been tested, lepidopterists assume that the startling effect of this snakelike pattern and behavior on a marauding bird may often act as a deterrent.

The principal means of defense in the pupal stage are the form and placement of the chrysalid. The orange-tip butterfly has a chrysalid that looks like a thorn jutting out from a twig. That of the zebra butterfly resembles a curled, drying leaf. The cocoon of the large tolype moth is spun on the concave side of a curved twig and matches the bark so closely that the twig looks just a little thickened. But for the most part a chrysalid is protected by its positioning out of the view of birds or beneath leaf litter or the soil's surface.

The adult moth or butterfly has both passive and active means of protection. Camouflage, in the form of blending with the surface or surroundings where the insect rests, is common. Many moths have barklike patterns on their forewings, which are usually exposed when the insects are roosting. The wings of anglewing butterflies are gaudy on top but the undersides resemble dead leaves. When the undersides of zebra butterfly wings are exposed, they show a pattern of light lines against dark, blending with the patterns of twigs in the thickets where the zebras roost in groups. Sallow moths, disturbed while feeding at sap runs, will drop to the leaf litter and lie motionless in whatever position they land, defying discovery.

Startle patterns are another strategy. Underwing moths, concealed by the cryptic color pattern of their forewings against the bark of a tree trunk, can suddenly expose their hindwings to reveal a banded pattern of yellow and black or red and black. Yellow/black and red/black are biological warning signals, used with validity by hornets, for example, but also by other insects for their startle value. (And consider the yellow or red "caution" and "stop" signs along our roadways.)

"Eyespots" are common among both moths and butterflies. Some lepidopterists speculate that eyespots are used by butterflies as a scare tactic and to protect critical parts of their bodies from injury. The suddenly un-covered hindwings of the io moth and of some of the sphinx moths display a pair of eyes much bigger than those of an investigating bird. In this re-gard, the great tropical owl butterfly is the most extreme example: the spread undersurfaces of the wings present a highly convincing imitation of a rather large owl's eyes. According to this theory, some of the smallest of butterflies, the hairstreaks, have a particularly ingenious defense. The butterfly rests with wings folded over the back and moves the hindwings alternately back and forth. The lower corner of the hindwing is decorated with a small eyelike spot; a fine hairlike tail protrudes from the edge of the wing. The motion draws attention to this portion of the wing so that an attacking bird or lizard, aiming for the "head" of its prey, ends up with a few bits of wing for its trouble, and the hairstreak flies off to live a little longer. Nectaring hairstreak and swallowtail butterflies are often observed to lack the lower corners of their hindwings.

Any collector of moths or butterflies will see many individuals bearing V-shaped marks of missing scales or V-shaped tears at the edge of the membrane on one or more wings. These are the marks of bird beaks, and their location indicates what the insect may have been doing at the time of attack: one wing, flying; two wings on one side, resting with wings laid down; symmetrical, on two or four wings, resting with wings folded up over the back.

The presence of these marks indicates that many Lepidoptera taken by birds manage to struggle free. The loosely attached, slippery wing scales make the capture of Lepidoptera by birds less easy than picking cherries. Many more butterflies avoid capture than escape from their grasp, how-ever. You need only to try capturing a flying butterfly with a net to appre-ciate its visual alertness and the speed with which it can change course to keep out of reach.

Bats present a particular problem, but noctuid moths have evolved a workable solution. The foraging bat emits bursts of sound waves at ultra-sonic frequencies (relative to human hearing) in order to echo-locate po-tential obstructions and to track flying insect prey. The noctuid moth has two ear cavities at the rear of the thorax, each containing just two nerve cells, which are receptive to the bat's echo-locating frequencies. When the moth hears high-intensity sound waves from the bat, it immediately dips into a zigzag dive to the ground, frequently eluding the bat. If the sound waves are low intensity, the moth flies away from the bat.

Even if captured by a bird, some butterflies have one more line of de-fense. Chemicals in the host plant eaten by the larvae and concentrated in the adult make some species unpalatable or even poisonous: the zebra but-terfly, from passion vine; the pipevine swallowtail, from pipe vine; the monarch and queen, from milkweed. Associating the unpleasant taste or immediate vomiting with eating these butterflies, birds learn to avoid any butterflies with their patterns and coloring.

Some butterfly species benefit from these distasteful species through mimicry. The viceroy, whose close relatives are mainly black, dark blue, and white, has evolved a color and pattern that pass at first glance for those of a monarch. In Florida, where the chocolate-colored queen butterfly is common, the viceroy has a mahogany, rather than orange, ground color in its wings. Many birds are unable to distinguish between the model and its mimics. A viceroy relative, the banded purple, is blue-black with a white band in the northern states. In the central and southern states, where the pipevine swallowtail flies, the white band is lost, the blue is enhanced, and the butterfly is called the red-spotted purple. At first glance the latter is easy to mistake for the pipevine swallowtail. In the southern part of the range, where it occurs with the pipevine swallowtail, the female tiger swallowtail is frequently black, rather than yellow, and is considered another mimic. The spicebush swallowtail may be another participant in this deceit.

These are but a few of the many devices that moths and butterflies use to defend their survival. For most species, the measure of success is that life goes on. But when a population is extinguished or a species becomes extinct, the chances are overwhelming that we, purporting to be sapient human beings, have tipped the balance through our ignorance or lack of concern.

European cabbage white (*Pieris rapae*) sipping nectar from globe amaranth or chafflower (*Gomphrena globosa*), Sarpy County, Nebraska. JOHN WEBER, JR.

The Life Cycle of the Large White Butterfly

~

Miriam Rothschild

*These strange and mystical transmigrations that I have
observed in Silkworms, turned my Philosophy into Divinity.*

THOMAS BROWNE

T HE LARGE WHITE BUTTERFLY is an exhibitionist almost all its
life. It snowflakes in the garden in spring sunshine and flaps
around the lavender and the cabbage patch in summer. It is the
most attractive and conspicuous insect in Great Britain. The female lays
batches of bright yellow torpedo-shaped eggs, fifty to a hundred or more,
which hatch into eye-catching caterpillars living gregariously on the surface of their food plant. Only the pupae are sometimes cryptic, and then
appear to match their background.

When insects adopt a self-advertising lifestyle, it is pretty safe to assume they are well protected by the presence of toxins or intensely bitter
substances in their bodily tissues. After one experience, predators avoid
these conspicuous butterflies. The large white is no exception, for during
its larval stages it sequesters and stores mustard oils, which are consumed

*From her home and laboratory in Peterborough, England, **Miriam Rothschild** shares these
life-history portraits of two butterfly species indigenous to her region and to the Eurasian continent: the large white and the European or small cabbage white. Although the European
cabbage white is now so well naturalized in North America that it is ubiquitous and sometimes
an agricultural pest, neither of these white butterfly species is indigenous to North America.
We note particularly that introduction to North America of the large white would pose serious*

Large white (*Pieris brassicae*) laying eggs. MIRIAM ROTHSCHILD

with its food plant, and in the pupal and adult stages it secretes a lethal protein (pierin).

Numerous entomologists have watched the courtship of the large white, but there is an odd divergence of opinion among them. Some say the male actively pursues the female; others maintain that the female actively courts the male. Certain observers believe the female raises her abdomen into a vertical position—like a policeman's truncheon—to signal refusal, while others insist this gesture is one of encouragement. I have seen it used exclusively to warn off the persistent, unwelcome male suitor.

ecological and agricultural problems. We urge all butterfly gardeners to propagate plants native to their regions and to encourage native plants and insects to flourish, rather than attempt to duplicate species lists from other regions. As David K. Northington of the National Wildflower Research Center notes in "Wildflowers in the Planned Landscape" (see page 111), placing butterfly gardens within the context of indigenous flora and fauna guards against the potentially harmful and unlawful introduction of nonnative plants and insects.

When the female acquiesces, the male achieves copulation by a rather sly, unobtrusive, lateral attack. In a garden growing semitropical flowers, butterflies are sometimes caught by the proboscis in the floral trap of a milkweed flower. In this helpless situation specimens of *both sexes* may be sexually assaulted by a free passing male.

Pairing lasts several hours, but if the mating butterflies are disturbed, the male flies away, carrying the female with him. During copulation not only sperm are passed into the female, but also a fluid containing a so-called egg-deterrent pheromone, which spreads over the eggs when they pass out along the oviduct. This volatile substance discourages other females from laying nearby and prevents the food plant of the future caterpillar from becoming overloaded.

Female large white (*Pieris brassicae*) caught by her proboscis in a bladder flower (*Araujia sericifera*) and mating with a male. MIRIAM ROTHSCHILD

The fertilized female supposedly ignores the appeal of flowers as her attention becomes centered exclusively on the color green and the shapes of leaves. But this is not strictly accurate, for on first awakening she seeks out flowers and nectars freely until about 10 A.M. She then sets out to search for a suitable oviposition site. She may also be attracted during the period of egg laying to the nectar of the cruciferous plants on which she deposits her eggs; the blooms seem to act as specific stimulants to oviposition. Sight, scenting, and touch determine the female's choice. She will drum and scratch with her forelegs on any green leaf which has attracted her, thus releasing chemical substances from the plant tissues which she assesses with tarsal nerve cells, or with her antennae, or, more rarely, with her proboscis.

Her behavior changes when she identifies mustard oils in the plant. These function for her as an oviposition cue, and she begins to search the plant for an ideal site, fluttering close to the surfaces of the leaves, touching them with her wings, and often pausing to drum again. While searching in a cabbage patch or along a hedgerow, the female drums, on an average, sixteen times before settling on a leaf, snapping her wings to, and cautiously curling her abdomen under the edge to lay the first egg. Her intensely quiet behavior is then in great contrast to her usual conspicuous flight style. Sometimes the feel of the underside of the leaf appears unsatisfactory. A nervous mechanism, initiated via sensory hairs at the end of the abdomen, then comes into play; and although the ovipositor may open, the passage of the egg is inhibited.

Why doesn't the female lay immediately after she has tested a leaf releasing mustard oils? It has been suggested that only an accumulation of satisfactory testings initiates oviposition, thus ensuring that sufficient host-plant material is available for her numerous brood. Mustard oils are also the feeding cue of the newly hatched caterpillars.

Many subsidiary factors determine the butterfly's choice of oviposition site. The color of the leaves, for instance—she will always prefer green to red cabbage leaves. The presence of other eggs acts as a deterrent, and so does foliage partially eaten or nibbled by slugs or other caterpillars, or leaves mottled by virus disease or damaged by aphids.

The eggs themselves are objects of great beauty, for their bright yellow shells are ridged and netted like a piece of modern sculpture. Their color is due to the presence of carotenoid pigments sequestered from the food plant by the larvae. If they are fed on a carotenoid-free diet, the eggs are pure white, not yellow; so is the silk with which the pupating caterpillar eventually secures itself to the substrate.

The eggs hatch in about ten days (the precise period determined by both temperature and humidity), and the emerging larvae first consume a large part of their eggshells and then arrange themselves in close proximity to one another on the leaf surface. They are aposematic (warningly colored): bright yellow or green, liberally speckled with black dots and dashes. If, however, one accidentally drops to the ground and lands in the debris of faded leaves beneath the plant cover, away from its fellows, it blends in well with the background and turns into a cryptic species almost impossible to detect. It is thus a good example of "dual signaling"—aposematic en masse and at close quarters but cryptic at a distance.

In the great majority of green caterpillars, their color is due to the mixing in the eye of the beholder of self-secreted blue bile pigments in close juxtaposition to the yellow carotenoids, which are both present in larval tissues—a physical, not a chemical, mixture. But the caterpillar of the white butterfly is an exception. Its basic yellow coloring is due to the presence of sepiapterin, and the integument is sufficiently transparent to allow the plant content of the gut to show through and provide the bright green coloration. Curiously enough, this species only secretes blue bile pigments in the last instar. The caterpillar sheds its skin four times before attaining full size.

If, while you are wandering through the garden, you pause and produce a fair imitation of a blackbird's or thrush's whistle, you can see the large white caterpillars on the surfaces of the leaves respond in unison by violently jerking the anterior, or front end, of their bodies from side to side. This is undoubtedly a communal defensive display, and similar behavior can be seen in aposematic, gregarious sawfly larvae on currant bushes. Does it frighten off small birds? One assumes it must have this effect.

Where are the caterpillars' ears? Not only in their heads, for, accidentally decapitated, they will still respond to a bird call in their vicinity by swinging their mutilated bodies from side to side.

The large white has many enemies and falls victim to tiny parasitic wasps, bacteria, and viruses, as well as various larger predators such as birds, harvestmen, spiders, hornets, and wasps. The latter are voracious enemies of larvae—stinging them before biting them up into manageable pieces for easy transport back to their nests.

When full grown, the caterpillar ceases to feed and initiates a wandering period, during which it seeks out a suitable site for pupation. It frequently selects a sheltered spot on a wall or fence or below a ledge or sill. There it spins a silken pad to which it hooks itself securely before casting its final larval skin. As a further precaution, a silken safety girdle is spun and looped around the middle portion to protect the emerging chrysalid.

At first the pupa is a bright emerald green with narrow yellow ridges, but then its color changes according to the light and background. If, for instance, the situation chosen is a cabbage leaf, the bile pigments and carotenoids are routed into the tissues immediately below the cuticle, and the chrysalid becomes dull cabbage green in tone. If the background is a gray stone wall, all the blue and yellow pigments are withdrawn into deeper tissues or, perhaps, destroyed, and the chrysalid becomes gray or silvery white with various degrees of black blotching. It is an interesting fact that on a carotenoid-free diet this withdrawal apparently cannot take place, for then, whatever the light conditions and color of the background may be, the bile pigments remain in the superficial tissues and the chrysalid is blue in color. Who will elucidate this mystery? Butterfly gardeners have a lot to occupy their minds while digging over their flower beds.

The chrysalid which results from a caterpillar feeding in late spring or early summer "cracks into shining wings" in about ten days, but offspring of the second brood overwinter in the pupal stages. Do they contain a glycerine-like antifreeze which protects them from the effects of frost? We do not know.

On a warm summer day you can sometimes see a nuptial flight of large whites rising and falling like a shattered Greek column above a pool. If you are very lucky, a big migratory movement may pass through the garden, a few feet above your head—a sparse snowstorm moving purposefully southward, rising steeply to negotiate the trees which bar their invisible flight line. But usually you see a solitary male apparently flapping aimlessly across your lawn, like a stray thought. . . .

> *Even the aerobatic swift*
> *has not his flying-crooked gift*
> ROBERT GRAVES

Within the last decade the large white has experienced the melancholy fate of becoming a laboratory tool. Furthermore, in schools in the United Kingdom it has replaced the frog as an object of study. More is known about it than any other butterfly, and no fewer than eight thousand papers have been devoted to the subject. The agricultural pest of yesterday has suddenly become an object of serious scientific research. But respect the large white—respect life! If you must dissect it in the pursuit of knowledge, always use an anesthetic. Maybe, instead, you will let it out the window.

The European cabbage white (*Pieris rapae*) lays single eggs.   RICHARD HUMBERT

The European or Small Cabbage White

The large white butterfly is not a North American species. Its next relative, the European or small cabbage white, takes its place. It has become so well naturalized since its first introduction (about 1860, near Montreal) that it is now ubiquitous. The European cabbage white is less well defended chemically than the large white, but it is nevertheless one of the most common butterflies in American gardens and just as delightful to watch and admire.

You can guess this species is less toxic, for it does not lay its eggs in batches and the caterpillars are green and cryptic and not markedly gregarious—the last instar buries itself, whenever the structure of its food plant permits, well out of sight in the heart of the cabbage. Nor do the caterpillars smell as revolting as those of the large white. If you watch the female closely when she is laying eggs (her choice of food plant is similar to that of the large white), you will see that she depends less on drumming and more on the sensory hairs at the tip of her abdomen for testing the suitability of the leaf she has selected.

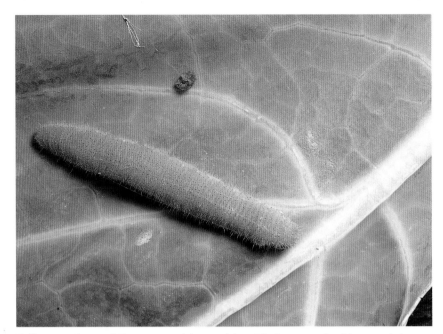

Full-grown larva of European cabbage white (*Pieris rapae*). At this stage it is often concealed in the heart of the cabbage (*Brassica oleracea*), Mill Valley, California.   EDWARD S. ROSS

Very much more is known about the habits of the European cabbage white than of the large white, owing chiefly to the excellent observations of American entomologists; nevertheless, a vast amount of information is still to be gained from watching this butterfly. For instance, the large white female does not lay her eggs on those few cruciferous plants which contain defensive heart poisons known as cardenolides as well as the oviposition cue of mustard oils. She recognizes these substances, which are present on the leaf surfaces, with one of the sensory cells in the soles of her feet. She has only to touch the leaf surface to know this plant is dangerous to her offspring. The European cabbage white, likewise, does not lay on the wall-flower and related species containing heart poisons. But how does she recognize their presence? We do not know.

Sometimes the large white performs a very strange act. It lands near an egg batch which has been laid on the surface of a cabbage leaf (this is not unusual in the field), puts its head on one side, extends its tongue, and draws it back and forth across the eggs like the bow of a violin. What is it testing or tasting? I have not the slightest idea. Does the European cabbage white perform similarly? If so, why? With a species as common as this delightful butterfly, the garden can be a laboratory or observatory as well as an area for growing flowers and attracting birds and insects.

Much insight into the lives of butterflies can be gained by just watching and recording. Which nectars probably contain the precursors of sex pheromones? What function do plant odors play in stimulating sexual intercourse? Where does the European cabbage white roost? Is it a semi-communal rooster like the large white? How does it know when a storm is in the offing?

There is immense pleasure to be gained by familiarizing oneself with the common species in the garden, and a certain amusement by keeping the knowledge gained to oneself, to be the only one who knows their private lives and, in a sense, shares them.

The eggs of the European cabbage white, which rim the leaves of the food plant, are said to be eaten by sparrows but are, even more frequently, taken by arthropods. Tits prey on older caterpillars and pupae, and thrushes and flickers hunt on the ground for wandering or dislodged caterpillars. Nevertheless, we are very ignorant about the natural enemies of butterflies and the diseases and changing conditions that control their numbers.

The European cabbage white is also a periodic migrant and wanderer, but which individuals leave your garden and return and which remain or arrive unexpectedly is a bit of a mystery. If you are curious about their movements, you can catch a number of specimens and mark them with a colored dye and try to watch. Once on the French coast I saw a large flight of European cabbage whites coming in across the sea. They were accompanied by dragonflies and even a few bees. Do they orient by the sun? Can they settle on the surface of the sea to rest and rise again? We do not know. Writers have envied "their untracked blue airway," but it may not be as untracked as it seems to the poets.

Today, the European cabbage white is often considered an agricultural pest. In China, for instance, I have seen *Pieris* present in incredible and formidable numbers. But the pest of today becomes the rarity of tomorrow. Gardeners are the potential friends and protectors of white butterflies; they should watch and wonder and be grateful.

> *Kill not the moth or butterfly*
> *For the last judgment draweth nigh.*
> WILLIAM BLAKE,
> "AUGURIES OF INNOCENCE"

Chrysalid of Mexican fritillary (*Euptoieta hegesia*).
STEVE PRCHAL, SONORAN ARTHROPOD STUDIES, INC.

Notes from a
Butterfly Gardener

~

Jo Brewer

TODAY, AS BUTTERFLY HABITATS are being persistently whittled away, we who greatly appreciate butterflies plant gardens for them. In so doing, we make a contribution to the continued existence of their small splendor.

The butterfly lover studies and protects butterflies—is awed by them and tries to be their friend. But in the end they fly away. Perhaps this carefree independence is what, in part, makes butterflies so appealing. They cannot be wheedled into perching on the windowsill each day at a particular hour. Rather, they charge through the garden like a wild roller coaster—up to a treetop, over the roof, and down to the meadow.

While we cannot confine them to one garden, we can lure them to our flowers. We can find their eggs and, in rearing them, study their habits and increase the numbers that survive. And we can bring our gardens to life by adding a new dimension to sun, wind, color, and change—the dimension of carefree flight.

Different species of butterflies have different lifestyles, and for this reason a butterfly garden needs to have a variety of habitats. A garden planted

Jo Brewer, a former long-standing board member of the Xerces Society, is a noted author, lecturer, and butterfly-gardening expert. An amateur lepidopterist, she worked for ten years as a research associate in the Insect Migration Studies program at the University of Toronto. In conjunction with that project, she reared and tagged approximately two thousand monarch butterflies. Jo Brewer is the coauthor, with her husband, Dave Winter, of Butterflies and Moths: A Companion to Your Field Guide *(Englewood Cliffs, N.J.: Prentice-Hall,*

with this in mind will attract more butterflies than a mere flower bed—in numbers, in variety, and in length of stay. We discovered this when we moved to our present house.

Within our boundaries are a marsh, a thicket, a woods, and a meadow, in addition to seven gardens, all rather small. All this covers an area of about an acre and a half. The house is built on a slight rise, with the Charles River flowing by just below it.

We call this house "Foggy Bottom" because every morning before sunrise the river is crowded with little mists that march along on the surface of the water as it winds slowly toward the edge of the city of Boston, just one mile away. When the sun rises out of its red and purple horizon, the mists rise also, like little ghosts, and silently disappear, leaving all of Foggy Bottom varnished with sunlight. From our dining-room window we see our back lawn and beyond it a thicket—a tangle of wild blackberry, wild grapevines, wild roses, and dogwood. Beyond the thicket lies the marsh, and beyond that, the river. When the river floods it drowns the marsh, but during a dry spell I can walk through it dry-shod, and along the path that leads to it, which, when in flood, would be up to my knees.

The path to the river is bordered with trees and wild shrubs. Trees arch over it, but at both ends the path is open, with trees only on its north side. This is an ideal situation for spicebush swallowtails, for this species patrols open areas under tree canopies.

A few years ago, owing to a rare bit of good luck, I witnessed a striking example of this behavior. I was visiting a friend in Chillicothe, Ohio, at the time. We were walking along a wooded path when we became aware that a spicebush swallowtail was patrolling the path for a distance of about fifteen yards, occasionally disappearing into the woods and then flying out again. After watching this action for a while, we realized that butterflies other than the one we had first seen were involved. We then stationed ourselves at points near the exits and entrances of the butterflies, signaling back and forth as to whether we had seen a male or a female. This was not easy to discern, but when it was possible to catch a quick glimpse of the hindwings we could usually tell, because the upper side of a female's wings are iridescent blue, while those of a male are gray-green. They all appeared to be males. Sometimes two would almost collide en route, and a third occasionally veered by. We were at a loss to know what was going on.

1986), and the author of Wings in the Meadow *(Boston: Houghton Mifflin, 1967), plus numerous articles on butterflies in magazines, including* Defenders of Wildlife, Horti-culture, Yankee, Down East, *and* Audubon. *She has lectured extensively before audiences of all ages, illustrating her talks with slides from her vast collection documenting the life history of some of our most fascinating butterflies. Portions of the following article have appeared in the Xerces Society's membership magazine* Wings.

Male spicebush swallowtail (*Papilio troilus*), Virginia. TOM PIERSON

Then all of a sudden, six of the butterflies came rushing down the roadway like a length of black ribbon in the wind. Just as they reached me the leader turned sharply into the woods, and the rest followed in a perfect curve: stunt pilots in miniature, showing off to giants!

In an instant they had vanished into the darkness of leaves. I often think of that sudden mass flight into the woods—its grace, its joyous freedom, its sudden perfection—and I can almost envision the butterfly that led the chase as having brilliantly blue hindwings, while those of her pursuers were a pale silvery green!

We acquired the two favorite larval food plants of the butterfly—a sassafras tree which we found in a wood, and a spicebush which we bought, and planted one at each end of the tunnel (where they face full sun but are protected from behind). Spicebush swallowtails have been residents ever since that time. We have found their eggs and their caterpillars on both the sassafras tree and spicebush every year. We have watched their black forewings cutting crescent-shaped streaks in the air and the shimmering blue and silver-green of their hindwings steering their erratic passage down the path in a mad chase as they take full advantage of our first butterfly habitat.

The Large River Garden and Its Inhabitants

The large river garden is a rectangle forty feet long and four feet wide planted with many popular butterfly nectar plants. In order to have continuous bloom throughout the months from early spring through late fall, we planted clumps of dame's rocket, garden phlox, and New England asters along the back edge of the garden.

These three plants, two wild and one cultivated, blossom in sequence from May to September and attract many butterflies (the most spectacular being the three New England swallowtails), many small skippers, and the hummingbird clearwing moth. The phlox is popular with many species both great and small, and the blooming time of the New England asters coincides with the arrival of the monarchs as they pass through Massachusetts on their way to Mexico in early fall.

Besides these three basic lures, we have planted red zinnias, which appeal to the monarchs, and yellow and orange marigolds. The yellow ones

Great spangled fritillary (*Speyeria cybele*) on swamp milkweed (*Asclepias incarnata*).   GEORGE O. KRIZEK, M.D.

were unsuccessful, but the orange marigolds attracted the first great span-gled fritillary ever seen on our property. This butterfly is a reliable resident in Maine year after year, but it is certainly a rarity in Dedham, Massachusetts!

I also sowed some seeds of a small plant we had found blooming on a heap of sand in Islesboro, Maine. This small annual, called *Centaureum pulcellum*, proved to be a great success. Its bright cerise-pink flowers bloom from June through September, and so far it has attracted a variety of small butterflies and skippers, as well as hummingbird clearwing moths, clouded sulfurs, and American painted ladies. It acts as a ground cover, spreading to fill empty spaces, seeds itself magnificently, and is not a troublemaker, as its roots are quite fragile.

We planted a corner of pearly everlasting, a favorite larval food of the American painted lady, and a large stand of pink turtlehead that we first thought would attract Baltimores, but we were doomed to disappoint-ment. The Baltimore, the state insect of Maryland, is also rather rare in our area. In fact we have seen only two, and we happened upon these as we walked along a power line cut about six miles from our house. The plant thrived, but butterflies showed no interest in it. Later we added more plants, including boneset, Joe-Pye-weed, and wild bergamot, all of which were highly successful.

About three years later we transplanted a small root of white turtle-head from Maine into the front part of the large river garden, and it thrived. When we returned from a vacation in Maine in mid-July a year later, I was astonished to find a nest spun around the plant and a colony of tiny Baltimore caterpillars avidly feeding on the leaves inside the nest!

It was impossible to count them, but when autumn came I saw that they had left the nest. I carefully separated the scraps of fallen leaves on the ground below and found a half-dozen or more of the little creatures hi-bernating. We left them to their own devices, hoping that their time clocks would mesh with those of the turtlehead.

When April came, we made a round of our gardens, especially the large river garden, and over the period of about a week we found three partly grown Baltimore caterpillars. Two lay dormant in curled leaf frag-ments near the white turtlehead which had not yet leafed out. The third was found on a leaf of the pink turtlehead, which was new-green and very tempting. It was about eighteen feet away from the other caterpillars. I thought that they would have a better chance of surviving if I took them indoors. Since one was already feeding on pink turtlehead, the others probably would be able to digest it also. All three caterpillars became full grown and ready to pupate, but two died before making their chrysalids.

The last one did pupate but died before the butterfly emerged. I really don't know why they died, and indeed they might have died anyway, but I think the loss of their preferred food plant may also have contributed to their demise.

Two years later the turtlehead was spreading. One day I noticed that other Baltimore larvae were feeding on the still-flourishing turtlehead. I happened to walk by it a month later and was astonished to see a newly emerged Baltimore butterfly in my garden for the first time. Such little victories provide such tremendous rewards!

Male black swallowtail (*Papilio polyxenes*) drinking nectar from lantana (*Lantana camara*).   JOHN R. RIGGENBACH

Female monarch (*Danaus plexippus*). FRANS LANTING

Plant Selection

Recommending flowers to attract butterflies in any given area is no easy task. We know what we would like to see in our gardens: irises, tulips, roses, and peonies. Unfortunately, this is not the case with butterflies. Butterflies are not interested in some of our most beloved blossoms. Finding flowers with great appeal to butterflies that are also acceptable to people is a challenge.

I planted two small clumps of golden Alexander in my garden, thinking it would be a host plant for black swallowtails. They never went near it, and I am still weeding it out from among the roots of my phlox and asters.

In Texas one year we saw a lantana shrub growing wild. It was covered with butterflies. This was an inspirational sight. When we returned to New England, we bought a pot of lantana and planted it in our garden. I didn't expect it would attract the swarms we had witnessed in Texas, but neither did I suspect that it would be ignored by all butterflies. It was! The point is, when you add wildflowers to your garden, it is better to purchase native plant species.

The common milkweed, one of the most important of all butterfly nectar plants, introduced itself into my butterfly garden. No gardener has ever been happier than I was when I saw its soft, almost silvery little blades pushing through the dark earth uninvited. This plant cannot be successfully transplanted with any ease because of its long taproot. But wherever it thrives, butterflies will find it. We have recorded eighteen species of New England butterflies nectaring at this plant, including the female monarch, which takes nectar from and lays her eggs on milkweed. Serious butterfly gardeners should make this flower a priority. It helps the monarchs in their autumn migration to wintering sites in California and Mexico and in their return to the North each spring.

Not all the butterflies that visit your garden will be on the same plants together. Nor will they all be in your garden together because they may not emerge at the same time, but a stand of milkweed in or near your garden will increase the number of visiting butterflies.

Milkweed is also known for the poisonous ingredients which monarchs sequester into their tissues as a protection against predation by birds. Its other hazard is not as well known. Each little blossom in the multiple flower heads of milkweed has at its center a biological device similar to the toy known as a Chinese finger trap. Anyone who has put a finger into one of these traps knows that pulling it out is exceedingly difficult! A worse problem is occasionally faced by insects nectaring on various milkweeds. I have found honeybees, wasps, flies, black ants, and one very small butterfly—a lycaenid—with feet or proboscis irrevocably snared in the traps of seemingly innocent milkweed flower heads.

The Question of Caterpillars

Caterpillars do not possess a single characteristic which would suggest to the uninitiated that they are related to butterflies or moths. They come in endless color combinations from pale green to black. Some are decorated with false faces which cause them to resemble snakes. Some pose as bird droppings. Some contain indigestible poisons, and some are equipped with tiny glands called osmeteria which, when extruded, resemble the tongues of snakes and, at the same time, give off an unpleasant odor. Some are smooth, some covered with spines or hairlike structures. Some contort themselves into ludicrous postures. Caterpillars—or larvae—have a presence which seems removed from reality.

They are often labeled worms because they are long and thin, and they crawl. To be a worm is to be ugly, disliked, and stepped on. This is a philosophy which every butterfly gardener must immediately reject. Although

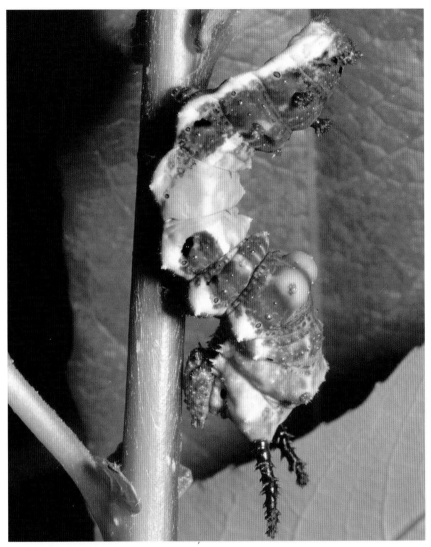

Lorquin's admiral larva (*Limenitis lorquini*) imitates bird dropping on willow (*Salix* sp.), Mill Valley, California.   EDWARD S. ROSS

caterpillars are long and thin, inside each one a butterfly or moth is being formed.

Only a few butterfly caterpillars actually cause significant destruction in the United States. One is the undistinguished little green larva of the European cabbage white butterfly, which was accidentally introduced into this country from Europe (see "The Life Cycle of the Large White But-

Larva of two-tailed swallowtail (*Papilio multicaudata*) displaying osmeteria.
STEVE PRCHAL, SONORAN ARTHROPOD STUDIES, INC.

First instar larva of pale swallowtail (*Papilio eurymedon*) eating its eggshell, Mill
Valley, California.   EDWARD S. ROSS

terfly," by Miriam Rothschild, page 43). It is a distinct pest to the farm gardener raising cabbage, broccoli, Brussels sprouts, or cauliflower. The others are the rather handsome larvae of the *Colias* butterflies, the common and orange sulfurs. These larvae are smooth gray-green with thin pink and white stripes on their sides. In some years they can overwhelm the alfalfa crop in parts of the West.

Caterpillars of most butterflies are not omnivorous feeders. They are astonishingly selective. Some species will feed on only one plant for their entire larval lives. The monarch is a classic example: this caterpillar eats nothing but plants in the milkweed family.

The young caterpillar chews a hole in its shell, nibbles away at bits of leaf, grows until it sheds its skin, and then becomes a second instar. When the process of shedding has taken place four or more times, the caterpillar will be in its fifth and last instar. It sheds its last larval skin, revealing a thimbleful of life with neither feet for walking nor wings to help it fly—a form reminiscent of a swaddled infant. Within twenty-four hours the delicate thin shell of the chrysalid will have dried and hardened.

The chrysalids of some butterflies are the jewels of the animal world. In these new costumes they are camouflaged by leaves and grasses and sunlight until the butterfly emerges. When this transformation is complete, the thin, transparent covering cracks open and a new creature tumbles out. Soft and helpless, it clings to the empty shell and waits.

Gone are the tiny eyes through which the caterpillar had barely been able to discern light from darkness, and in their place are the marvelous multifaceted orbs that transmit a broad spectrum of colors and motions from all directions. Gone are the caterpillar's mandibles and the spinneret used to make the delicate carpet of silk that had been its bed. Now there is a long, coiled proboscis that many of the new creatures will use to probe into the hearts of flowers for nectar.

But more miraculous than any of these are the insect's wings—the tiny, crumpled wings no bigger than a fingernail, the fourfold cloak of many colors which unfolds and stretches and smooths as all the veins of the wings fill with fluid, which in some species is a transparent emerald green.

And there it hangs, clinging to its shell, alone and defenseless, waiting for the wing veins to become firm enough to support it in flight.

There it waits, somewhere between earth and sky, vulnerable to all the insect diseases, all the vagaries and violence of the weather, but, when this last ritual of metamorphosis has been completed, ready for the freedom of the air.

Female cloudless sulfur (*Phoebis sennae*) on wild senna pod (*Cassia* sp.), Holms County, Florida.   GARY RETHERFORD

Other Lures

Butterflies don't feed only on nectar. I first noticed this when I saw a viceroy sucking up juices from the carcass of a dead rabbit. Other species have been found on dead snakes and frogs and many other animals, as well as on their droppings.

Groups of butterflies are often seen drinking from damp soil or sand on the borders of ponds and streams. This is because the sand contains salts and traces of materials from dead animals or animal excretions.

Male echo blues (*Celastrina argiolus echo*) on mud. When one alights, others join to imbibe moisture, Mill Valley, California.   EDWARD S. ROSS

The best place I found for photographing butterflies was a polluted stream running through a farmyard in Ecuador. I spent a morning there photographing butterflies I have never seen anywhere else. It was not the ideal spot for relaxed enjoyment of the countryside, but the point is that picking a spot in a sunny but unobtrusive place in your own yard for testing various butterfly recipes is not a bad idea. Overripe fruit makes an excellent lure, and simple banana mash is tough to beat. Any fermented fruit can be combined with wine or beer and a little honey or sugar. Experiment and see what happens. Pouring some of the brew over a sandy spot and keeping it damp may be a real treat for both you and the butterflies.

Introducing a Species

Introducing a butterfly species in a location where it does not normally occur is a widely discussed subject. Professional lepidopterists oppose this practice for several reasons:

～ If the species to be introduced is closely related to a species already established in the area, the two might interbreed, and the native species might eventually lose its identity and become extinct in the area. This could happen, if, for example, an anise swallowtail should be brought from California, where it is a native, to New England, where the black swallowtail is native and abundant. Both species eat wild carrots. Their eggs and caterpillars are, to all intents and purposes, identical. The chrysalids of both species vary in color and perhaps very slightly in shape. But the adults of both species are vastly different in pattern, shape, and habits.

An even greater problem would be the introduction of a foreign subspecies that would water down the locally selected genes of the native species, perhaps to its detriment.

～ If an introduced species has no known parasites or predators in the new area, its numbers could increase to overwhelming proportions. If its larval food plant is scarce and it switches to a similar plant utilized by native butterflies, some individuals of the native species could starve.

～ If the larval food plant of the introduced species is a plant used as food by people, the introduction of that species may cause massive damage, as the imported cabbage white did.

～ Introducing butterflies into areas where they don't naturally occur could interfere with natural distributional patterns and therefore confuse the study of butterfly biogeography.

Great Expectations?

When I look around my garden and see only one little skipper and a cabbage butterfly, I ask myself, "What have I done wrong?" Then I may realize that the flowers have not yet recovered from a severe winter frost or that a large cloud is beginning to cover the sun.

At times like these, I understand I have no real control over butterflies. If all the negative factors of a particular day go away, and the butterflies begin to appear, it is because they are in charge around here—not I.

So I am content to wander from one garden to another and see a spicebush swallowtail nectaring at bee balm or butterfly weed, a tiger swallowtail in and out of my orange daylilies, an anglewing or a red-spotted purple sipping from a patch of damp soil at the end of the drive. And when I do, it will be like all the other times—a moment of perfect beauty and grace.

Some people claim to have seen dozens of butterflies around a particular plant in their gardens. However, it is unlikely to happen every day, or

Male red-spotted purple (*Limenitis arthemis astyanax*) at moist sand, Seneca, Maryland.   GEORGE O. KRIZEK, M.D.

even every year. Random chance determines when one butterfly or another will suddenly appear in very large numbers.

I have never seen a large congregation of butterflies in my own garden, but I have seen five or six species flying the same day. I have also seen three spicebush swallowtails flying at once. They were performing a dance—changing position and direction and the angle of their wings all at once in a way no other butterfly can emulate.

In the course of four summers, my husband and I have recorded forty-one species of butterflies in our gardens and woods. We have reared fifteen species found either as young hibernating caterpillars or as eggs and larvae of butterflies that had already emerged.

A butterfly garden is not at its best if the only goal in mind is to attract hordes of butterflies. The true pleasures are memories that endure long after the butterflies have been buried under a frigid blanket of snow. An event witnessed once in a lifetime can be relived year after year as long as flowers bloom and memories endure.

Cloudless sulfur (*Phoebis sennae*) taking nectar from a hibiscus (*Hibiscus* sp.). JOHN R. RIGGENBACH

Butterfly Garden Design
~
Garden Concepts and Designs
by Mary Booth
Text by Melody Mackey Allen

W HAT IS BUTTERFLY GARDENING? In our complex world, the answer is temptingly simple: butterfly gardening is the art of growing plants that will attract butterflies. Few garden projects are easier, and few offer greater delight. In urban areas butterfly gardening is a regenerative activity, evoking in us a nearly forgotten sense of wonder.

Why Garden Design?

Nectar sources and larval food plants attract butterflies to gardens. Butterflies are indifferent to garden styles and aesthetics; people, however, are attracted to gardens primarily for the enrichment they afford. Using the basic concepts and designs presented in this section, you can create a butterfly garden that both you and a butterfly can appreciate.

A wide range of plant materials is suggested here, but you will want to limit your choices. If you do not, a butterfly garden can become a hodgepodge of unrelated colors and textures, and by midsummer, an overgrown, unruly tangle. You can avoid this by practicing a few simple design

Mary Booth is a landscape architect who has practiced in Anchorage, Alaska, and Seattle, Washington. Melody Mackey Allen is executive director of the Xerces Society. She is a former independent conservation consultant, Oregon Nature Conservancy consultant, and coauthor, with Dave Bohn, of Eight Dollar Mountain, An Essay *(Portland, Ore.: The Nature Conservancy, 1984).*

techniques. Trees, flowers, and shrubs have different growth rates, foliage, colors, and blooming sequences which can be combined effectively to attract a wealth of butterflies from spring to fall, as well as delight the eye of the gardener throughout most of the year.

Planning a Butterfly Garden

These ideas and suggestions are designed to spark the creative process. Design possibilities are unlimited and need not conform to any particular style, so you are free to create your own special vision.

A butterfly garden can be a little plot planted with a few nectar flowers or a large garden planted with great arrays of diverse nectar flowers for adult butterflies and food plants for their larvae. The first step is to give some thought to your garden setting and your own expectations. Consider

Male golden skipper (*Poanes taxiles*).   WILLIAM B. FOLSOM

the following questions; then, based on your answers, decide how to get started.

~ Which species of butterflies are in your area, and which plants do they use for nectar and larval food? Observe not only your yard, but your neighborhood and its surroundings as well. (See "Butterfly-Watching Tips," by Robert Michael Pyle, page 127.) Find out which butterflies are in the woods, meadows, waste spaces, abandoned railways, and other un-developed areas. Three days in the field may save you three months of fruit-less planting. Make a list of the butterflies you see and the flowers they are visiting. You will then be on your way to finding out what valuable flowers you already have in your yard, and what to plant for the species of butter-flies you particularly want to attract.

~ Examine the garden area you have. Can you see it from your living room or your kitchen? From a porch or patio? From lawn chairs? Will it be viewed from the street? Will children and pets be playing where the butterflies browse for nectar? The ideal place is undisturbed yet open to your view.

~ Butterflies are cold-blooded and need sunlight to warm the mus-cles they use to fly. Evaluate your garden's orientation. Does it receive enough sun? Keep track of the sun's position throughout the day in rela-tion to the gardening area. Based on your observations, do you need to move plants to provide more sun?

~ Butterflies also need wind protection. Do you need to add tall plants to buffer the wind?

~ Decide how much time you want to spend maintaining your gar-den. Do you want to devote your entire garden to butterflies or integrate butterfly plants into the rest of your garden? Assess your priorities by weighing the amount of maintenance you are willing to do, the require-ments of butterflies and the plants you choose, and the other gardening activities you enjoy. Bear in mind that the fewer pesticides used in or near your butterfly garden, the more success you will have. The ideal setting for your butterfly garden would be pesticide-free.

~ Evaluate your garden style. Does it seem informal, with curvilin-ear layouts and asymmetrical arrangements of shrubs, flowers, and trees which blend varied colors and textures? Or does it tend to be formal, with precise lines, structured or symmetrical organization, and shrubs and plantings arranged by color and in geometric shapes? You probably will want to match your new butterfly garden to the style of the rest of your garden.

Female queen (*Danaus gilippus*) on lantana (*Lantana camara*).   PETER J. BRYANT

Gardens and gardeners develop gradually. It is possible to begin butterfly gardening on a small scale and experiment with the process step by step. If you want to take it slowly, you can begin with one sunny, wind-protected bed the first year and plant a selection of three or four nectar plants which will bloom throughout the summer. Try bee balm, butterfly bush, and summer phlox. The next year you can increase the number of nectar plant selections and lengthen the blooming period to span the seasons from spring through fall. Try adding one or two common larval food plants, such as parsley or dill for swallowtails, or arugula, a favorite Italian salad green, for the cabbage white. In the third year, increase the number of nectar plant species again and experiment with less-familiar, indigenous larval and nectar plants from your local native plant nurseries.

Color

Butterflies do not care one whit about how you coordinate the colors you choose for your flower beds, but as summer progresses, you may. Late-summer flower beds can look like a painter's drop cloth; yet with care in their layout, they can also resemble a colorful tapestry. The needs of butterflies should be your primary guide; how you group colors depends on your particular vision. You may decide on a variety of color schemes throughout your yard.

The designs that follow suggest one basic set of colors. We have also added foliage plants so you can see how the colors of both flowers and foliage work together.

In order to create a unified visual effect, select the majority of flowers from either the warm color range (red, orange, yellow) or cool color range (purple, blue, white). Smaller quantities of contrasting colors can then be used to provide interest. You may want to include a sequence that begins with strong, basic colors and gradually tones down to pastel shades. Be prepared to experiment with different combinations. Some people find it helpful to draw and color a sketch of their garden as they plan.

Some general thoughts: Warm colors are showy and have a greater impact in the garden when they are seen against a strong green background. Cool colors are restful and subdued and work best if you add a white con-

Milbert's tortoiseshell (*Nymphalis milberti*) on French marigold (*Tagetes patula*).
JIM MESSINA, PRAIRIE WINGS

trast for freshness and brightness. Blue and white, for example, are extremely effective in early evening, when they seem to glow. The color of your background foliage can enhance flower colors. Soft gray background foliage brings pinks and mauves to life. Deep, rich green foliage intensifies reds and yellows.

Whether you choose warm or cool flower colors, you can add limited amounts of flowers with contrasting colors. With warm colors such as oranges and reds use cool colors such as purple or blue; with cool colors use yellow. You can use white or silver for contrast with either warm or cool colors. Adding contrast accentuates all colors, making them livelier and more prominent. The most important consideration is not to overdo the amount of contrast.

Larva of giant swallowtail (*Papilio cresphontes*), Big Thicket State Park, Texas.
GARY RETHERFORD

Small Butterfly-Garden Layouts

Diagrams 1 and 2 divide the garden into three main areas:

~ *The background area (also illustrated in Diagram 3).* This area uses foliage to provide a basic structure for the garden, a visual framework and a backdrop for the flowers. Frequently termed "foundation" plantings, these plants remain in place over the years. They consist of shrubs or small trees; some can be evergreen to give year-round structure, others deciduous; and they may be flowering or foliage plants. The background can also be a fence or wall covered with vines. Whatever its form, this background area can be planted to act as a screen to buffer nectaring butterflies from the prevailing winds. Butterfly-attracting shrubs such as abelia, butterfly bush, and wax-leaf privet are excellent choices. A number of trees are good larval food sources: willows, dogwoods, spicebush, and various fruit trees, for example (see Appendix B).

As a general rule, your choice of background plantings depends on your garden style. If your garden is informal, these shrubs and trees will grow in their natural, unpruned forms; have an irregular outline of height, shape, and color; and consist of a variety of foliage types. If your garden is formal, this planting will be geometric in shape and have a single foliage color and a consistent texture, such as that of a clipped evergreen hedge.

~ *The intermediate area.* The visual focal point of the planting bed, this is the stage for butterfly drama. It consists of colorful midsize to tall nectar flowers—perennials or annuals—planted in clusters of the same species to create a mass of blooms. Planting several plants of each nectar flower and planning for a sequence of blooms throughout the growing season will attract the widest variety of butterflies on the wing.

~ *The foreground area.* This planting defines the front boundary of the flower garden and requires low-growing plants so as not to block the larger nectar plant flowers in the intermediate area. These plants are placed close enough together to form an edge or border at the front of the bed, either in a soft line for an informal garden style or in a distinct edge for a formal garden. Plants for this area can be butterfly attracting, decorative, or both. They can be permanent, evergreen border plants—small shrubs and ground covers such as dwarf potentilla, St. John's wort, and trimmed honeysuckle. Or they can be low-growing perennials or annuals such as dwarf lavender, impatiens, sweet alyssum, and miniature marigolds.

Use the diagrams as a step-by-step guide to planting. You can repeat elements of any diagram in order to span a greater area.

DIAGRAM 1:
A Small Butterfly Garden

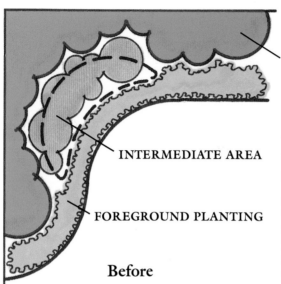

BACKGROUND PLANTING

INTERMEDIATE AREA

FOREGROUND PLANTING

Before

You can adapt an existing flower bed to create a small butterfly garden. This garden design consists of three areas: a background planting of evergreen and deciduous shrubs, trees, or vines, which provides a permanent backdrop for the nectar flowers; a foreground planting, which acts as a low border in front of the garden; and an intermediate area of nectar flowers.

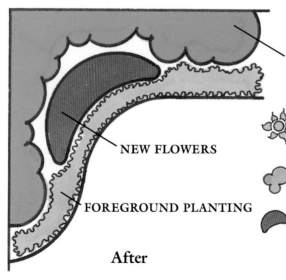

BACKGROUND PLANTING

NEW FLOWERS

FOREGROUND PLANTING

After

1. Choose a sunny, protected spot. If necessary, add tall, dense background plants to buffer the wind.

2. Remove existing plants from intermediate area.

3. Replant intermediate area with butterfly-attracting plants. (See Diagram 2; the Master Plant List provides additional suggestions.)

DIAGRAM 2:
Flower Placement for a Small Butterfly Garden

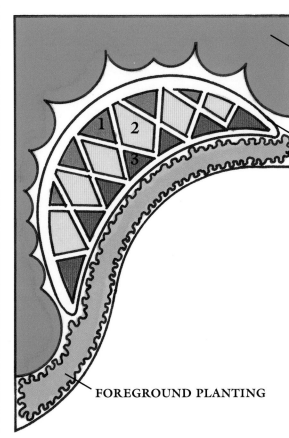

BACKGROUND PLANTING

INTERMEDIATE AREA

FOREGROUND PLANTING

The intermediate area consists of three rows divided into triangular or diamond-shaped sections. The size of the sections depends on the size of the area.

Suggested intermediate plants:

- **Row 1** contains the tallest plants: *Achillea filipendulina* (fernleaf yarrow) 'Coronation Gold', mustard yellow, 42 inches.
- **Row 2** contains plants of medium height: *Rudbeckia fulgida* (black-eyed Susan) 'Goldquelle', gold, 30 inches.
- **Row 3** contains the lowest plants: *Asclepias tuberosa* (butterfly weed), orange, 24 inches.

If you are starting a new garden or want to add to one, you may wish to use these plants:

Background plants: *Eleagnus pungens* (silverberry),* *Cotoneaster francheti* (cotoneaster),* *Salix* spp. (willows); prune willow to control its size.

Foreground plants: *Hypericum calycinum* (creeping St. John's wort),* *Potentilla fruticosa* (shrubby cinquefoil or poten-tilla) 'Tangerine' (prune to keep low), *Lonicera japonica* (Japanese honey-suckle), *Lantana* spp. (orange colors).

*Not butterfly attracting; use solely for purposes of design.

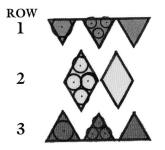

ROW

1

2

3

DIAGRAM 3:

DIAGRAM 3:
A Large Butterfly Garden

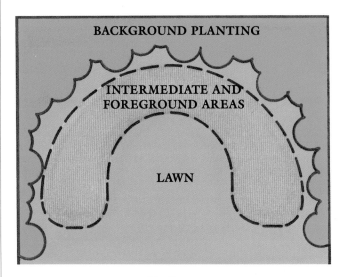

Before

This large garden features a variety of flowers, shrubs, and small trees that attract butterflies. It divides the intermediate and foreground areas into four rows. Plants are arranged in large clusters within the rows and increase in height from foreground to background.

1. Choose a sunny, protected spot.

2. Remove existing plants (or lawn) from both intermediate and foreground areas.

3. Add new background shrubs, using nectar or larval plants listed in Appendices A and B or the Master Plant List.

4. Replant intermediate and foreground areas with butterfly-attracting plants (see Diagram 4; the Master Plant List provides additional suggestions). When planting the rows, start from the back and work forward, row by row, cluster by cluster.

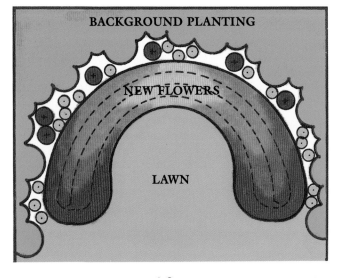

After

 New nectar shrub

 New larval shrub

A Large Butterfly-Garden Layout

You can extend the basic concept of background, intermediate, and foreground areas to create a large butterfly garden. Diagrams 3 and 4 show you how to weave a wide variety of plant materials together to produce a garden with a tapestry-like appearance. This design is based on English perennial gardens and combines many different butterfly-attracting flowers, which should coax a greater diversity of butterflies into your garden. The flowering plants are laid out in large clusters in four elliptical rows. The design can be applied to a typical 50-by-100-foot city lot, or any of the elements can be repeated to fill a bigger garden. Planting numerous clusters of several different nectar flowers may seem complicated, but the task is made manageable by taking it step by step and referring to the diagrams.

Grooming

Grooming is pruning, pinching back, clipping, removing dead flower heads, and cutting plants back. It is the fine-tuning process of gardening. We suggest you consult a good general gardening book to learn the basic techniques (see the Selected Bibliography). Here are some hints to increase the blooming capacity of your butterfly garden:

~ *Pinching back.* In mid to late spring, pinch back stems before the plant sets flower buds. With pinching back, many perennials and annuals will be bushier and produce more flowers. Examples of plants to pinch back are phlox, asters, most daisy-flowered plants, marigolds, ageratum, and bee balm.

~ *Deadheading.* As blooms fade, remove the dead flower heads. Deadheading prolongs the blooming time and increases the number of blooms per plant.

~ *Cutting back.* After spring- and early-summer-flowering perennials and annuals have finished their blooming cycles, cut them back to keep the plant from looking unkempt, to force new foliage, and, sometimes, to encourage a second blooming cycle. In late fall, cut any remaining perennials back to within three inches of the ground. Exceptions are plants whose winter form or seed pods offer visual interest through the winter, such as some irises, sedums, and ornamental grasses.

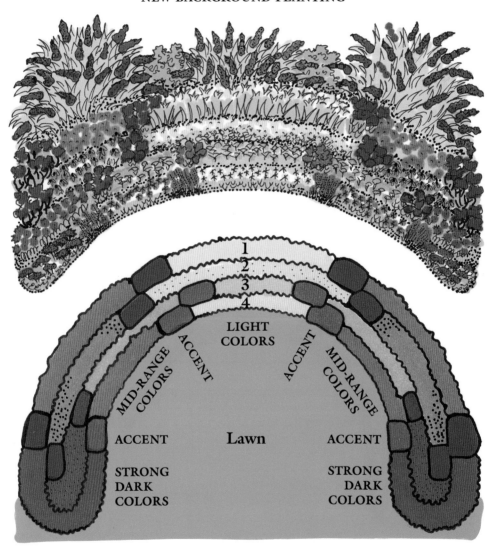

DIAGRAM 4:
Flower Placement for a Large Butterfly Garden

NEW BACKGROUND PLANTING

1
2
3
4

LIGHT
COLORS

ACCENT

MID-RANGE
COLORS

ACCENT

MID-RANGE
COLORS

ACCENT   Lawn   ACCENT

STRONG
DARK
COLORS

STRONG
DARK
COLORS

Plant List Key for Diagram 4

Many flowering plants are available in more than one color. Examples are garden phlox and bee balm, which come in colors ranging from deep purple to lavender, red to pink, and white. Daylilies and sneezeweed come in colors from rust to orange, gold to light yellow, and cream. Before choosing plants, develop your color scheme; then select plants according to both color and height. The Master Plant List identifies species and their typical flower colors but does not include all possible forms and colors. Consult the appendices of this book, as well as local nurseries and mail-order catalogs, to see what is available and appropriate for your region.

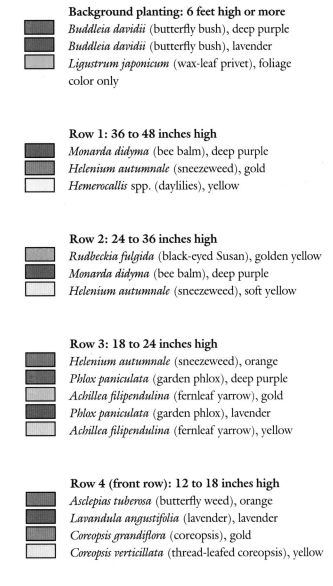

Background planting: 6 feet high or more

Buddleia davidii (butterfly bush), deep purple
Buddleia davidii (butterfly bush), lavender
Ligustrum japonicum (wax-leaf privet), foliage color only

Row 1: 36 to 48 inches high

Monarda didyma (bee balm), deep purple
Helenium autumnale (sneezeweed), gold
Hemerocallis spp. (daylilies), yellow

Row 2: 24 to 36 inches high

Rudbeckia fulgida (black-eyed Susan), golden yellow
Monarda didyma (bee balm), deep purple
Helenium autumnale (sneezeweed), soft yellow

Row 3: 18 to 24 inches high

Helenium autumnale (sneezeweed), orange
Phlox paniculata (garden phlox), deep purple
Achillea filipendulina (fernleaf yarrow), gold
Phlox paniculata (garden phlox), lavender
Achillea filipendulina (fernleaf yarrow), yellow

Row 4 (front row): 12 to 18 inches high

Asclepias tuberosa (butterfly weed), orange
Lavandula angustifolia (lavender), lavender
Coreopsis grandiflora (coreopsis), gold
Coreopsis verticillata (thread-leafed coreopsis), yellow

Male pale swallowtail (*Papilio eurymedon*) on trumpet honeysuckle (*Lonicera ciliosa*).   THOMAS C. BOYDEN

Conservation Considerations

Butterfly gardening is a simple, satisfying process. Still, before you begin, consider the following:

~ Don't transplant native plant species into your garden from the wild. Most native plants which attract butterflies are available through special nurseries; see "Resources" to locate such a nursery in your area. Not only will you have better luck working with nursery stock, but you will also be preserving your local native plant species and habitats. Such sensitivity to conservation is a valuable contribution to maintaining biological diversity in North America (see "Butterfly Gardening and Conservation," by Stanwyn G. Shetler, page 107, and "Wildflowers in the Planned Landscape," by David K. Northington, page 111).

~ If you plant wildflower seeds, be careful to purchase seed species native to your area of the country. In general, these seeds will germinate and grow better than species native to other areas. But more important, introducing wildflowers from outside a geographic area can upset the botanical apple cart. A pleasing native plant in one area of the country can become a menace in another—an invasive, destructive weed which overtakes native meadows, grasslands, or marshes if the new conditions encourage it to grow too prolifically. Most ecological invasions occur innocently enough with the planting of just a few specimens, but years later the plant is everywhere, destroying important plant communities.

~ We urge you to exercise caution in incorporating some plants. Morning glories, wild honeysuckles, blackberries, nettles, Bermuda grass, thistles, tansy, and similar plants will also invade and take over, though they are good nectar or larval food sources and aren't listed as noxious weeds. Some good nectar plants have extremely poisonous fruits or leaves. Weigh the risks. Nettles and thistles should not be allowed to spread and should be planted in tubs to contain their root systems. Their flower heads should be removed after blooming so the wind doesn't spread silk or seeds far and wide.

We have provided lists, instructions, caveats, and diagrams to facilitate butterfly gardening, but the two most important ingredients are the enthusiasm and the unique creativity of each gardener. It is our hope that butterfly gardens will appear in every neighborhood across America, and that people will find themselves spellbound as they observe the biological drama of insect life playing just outside their doorsteps.

MASTER PLANT LIST

The Master Plant List includes thirty flowering plants that butterflies use for nectar and, in some cases, larval food. This list represents our first choice of plants for a butterfly garden: they are widely available flowers that, in addition to being attractive to butterflies and humans and very easily grown, are functional and versatile within our suggested garden designs. However, this list represents only a fraction of the plants from which a butterfly gardener can choose. For a more complete listing of plants butterflies use for nectar and larval food and their geographical distribution, see Appendices A and B.

Both scientific and common names of plants may vary with different authors, time periods, or geographic regions. In compiling this list we have attempted to refer to plants by their most current and widely used names, and for some species we include more than one common name. Three scientific family names in this list have widely used alternates: Asteraceae (Compositae), Lamiaceae (Labiatae), and Brassicaceae (Cruciferae).

Photo identifications and credits appear on pages 185–186.

Abelia × *grandiflora*   (glossy abelia)
Family Caprifoliaceae   (honeysuckle)

TYPE: semievergreen shrub
HEIGHT: 5 feet or more
FLOWER COLOR: pale pink

BLOOM SEASON: summer to early fall
EXPOSURE: full sun to light shade
SOIL: well drained

Small, glossy leaves. In its natural shape or as a pruned hedge, can be used as background shrub to give structure to garden. Loses leaves in cold winter climates.

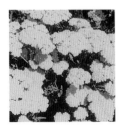

Achillea filipendulina   (fernleaf yarrow)
Family Asteraceae   (sunflower or composite)

TYPE: hardy perennial
HEIGHT: 3 to 4 feet
FLOWER COLOR: golden yellow

BLOOM SEASON: late summer to fall
EXPOSURE: full sun
SOIL: tolerates poor soil

Easy to grow from seed; flowers in second year. Good in mixed perennial garden. Fernlike foliage. Excellent dried or cut flower. Additional species: *A. ptarmica* (sneezeweed), white, 1 to 2 feet; *A. millefolium* (common yarrow, milfoil), white to red, 18 inches.

Asclepias tuberosa   (butterfly weed, orange milkweed)
Family Asclepiadaceae   (milkweed)

TYPE: hardy perennial	**BLOOM SEASON:** summer
HEIGHT: to 3½ feet	**EXPOSURE:** full sun
FLOWER COLOR: orange	**SOIL:** well drained, sandy

Fragrant; good cut flower. Good mass-planted in mixed perennial garden. Additional species: *A. incarnata* (swamp milkweed); *A. speciosa* (showy milkweed).

Aster × frikartii   (Frikart aster)
Family Asteraceae   (sunflower or composite)

TYPE: hardy perennial	**BLOOM SEASON:** late summer to
HEIGHT: 2 to 3 feet	fall
FLOWER COLOR: lavender with	**EXPOSURE:** full sun
yellow center	**SOIL:** well drained

Fragrant; good as individuals or mass-planted in mixed perennial garden. Additional species: *A. novae-angliae* (New England aster), violet; *A. novi-belgii* (New York aster), bright blue-violet. *A. novi-belgii* and other leafy-stemmed aster species are called Michaelmas daisies and are available in white and many shades of pink, red, purple, and blue.

Buddleia davidii   (orange-eye butterfly bush, summer lilac)
Family Loganiaceae   (logania)

TYPE: deciduous shrub	**BLOOM SEASON:** mid- or late
HEIGHT: 8 to 15 feet	summer to early fall
FLOWER COLOR: lavender/	**EXPOSURE:** full sun
purple with orange eye	**SOIL:** tolerates poor soil

Background-area foundation shrub. Stiff and upright, branching into arching shoots with 8-by-2-inch flower spikes. Requires deadheading to promote long blooming season. Also requires cutting back in late winter or early spring to within 12 inches of ground. Many named varieties; a few are dwarf/compact.

Centranthus ruber   (Jupiter's-beard, red valerian)
Family Valerianaceae   (valerian)

TYPE: perennial
HEIGHT: 2 to 3 feet
FLOWER COLOR: muted rose /
  pale red

BLOOM SEASON: summer to fall
EXPOSURE: full sun
SOIL: tolerates poor soil

Fragrant, vigorous plant which reseeds itself. Control spreading by deadheading. Can be mass-planted in mixed perennial garden.

Chrysanthemum spp.   (daisies)
Family Asteraceae   (sunflower or composite)

TYPE: hardy perennial
HEIGHT: 1 to 3 feet
FLOWER COLOR: yellow center
  with purple, violet, white, or
  reddish petals

BLOOM SEASON: all summer
EXPOSURE: full sun, partial
  shade
SOIL: moist, well drained

The wildflower *C. leucanthemum* (ox-eye daisy) is a common nectar source for butterflies. *C. maximum* and *C.* × *superbum* (sold as Shasta daisies) are widely available species. Good as individuals or mass-planted in mixed perennial garden. Selecting early-blooming varieties may extend bloom period.

Cosmos bipinnatus   (cosmos)
Family Asteraceae   (sunflower or composite)

TYPE: annual
HEIGHT: 4 to 10 feet
FLOWER COLOR: magenta,
  pink, or white with yellow
  center

BLOOM SEASON: late summer to
  fall
EXPOSURE: full sun
SOIL: tolerates poor soil

Tall and wiry; can be mass-planted in mixed perennial garden. Good cut flower.

Echinacea purpurea   (purple coneflower)
Family Asteraceae   (sunflower or composite)

TYPE: hardy perennial
HEIGHT: 2 to 4 feet
FLOWER COLOR: rose-purple
  with dark, raised center

BLOOM SEASON: midsummer to
  fall
EXPOSURE: full sun
SOIL: well drained

A native wildflower in Midwest and South, suited to hot, dry locations. Good dried or cut flower. Tolerates drought. Many cultivars with various colors and forms are available.

Eupatorium spp.   (Joe-Pye-weeds)
Family Asteraceae   (sunflower or composite)

TYPE: hardy perennial
HEIGHT: 2 to 3 feet
FLOWER COLOR: shades of rose

BLOOM SEASON: late summer to fall
EXPOSURE: full sun, light shade
SOIL: moist

Native to eastern U.S.; good cut flower. Can be used in mixed perennial garden. Native species include: *E. fistulosum* (hollow Joe-Pye-weed or trumpet weed); *E. maculatum* (spotted Joe-Pye-weed, smokeweed); *E. purpureum* (sweet or green-stemmed Joe-Pye-weed)—all are good butterfly plants, appear quite similar, and grow to 10 feet, shades of rose; *E. coelestinum* (hardy ageratum or mist-flower), blue.

Helianthus spp.   (sunflowers)
Family Asteraceae   (sunflower or composite)

TYPE: annual, perennial
HEIGHT: 3 to 10 feet
FLOWER COLOR: golden yellow
    with dark center

BLOOM SEASON: mid- to late summer
EXPOSURE: full sun
SOIL: tolerates poor soil

Smaller perennial sunflowers can be used in mixed perennial garden. The annual tall sunflower also produces edible seeds, prized by many birds.

Heliotropium arborescens   (heliotrope, cherry-pie)
Family Boraginaceae   (borage)

TYPE: half-hardy perennial
HEIGHT: 1½ to 4 feet
FLOWER COLOR: dark violet to
    white

BLOOM SEASON: late spring to summer
EXPOSURE: sun, light shade
SOIL: well drained

A common bedding plant. Can be mass-planted in mixed perennial garden. Vanilla-scented herb with colorful foliage.

Hemerocallis spp.   (daylilies)
Family Liliaceae   (lily)

TYPE: hardy perennial
HEIGHT: 3 feet
FLOWER COLOR: off-white, yellow, gold, orange, red, mahogany

BLOOM SEASON: summer
EXPOSURE: full sun
SOIL: well drained

Can be mass-planted in one color or a range of colors in mixed perennial garden. Nurseries often provide premixed colors.

Lantana camara   (lantana, yellow sage, hedgeflower)
Family Verbenaceae   (vervain)

TYPE: half-hardy shrub, vine
HEIGHT: to 6 feet
FLOWER COLOR: yellow, orange, red

BLOOM SEASON: summer, or all year in warm climates
EXPOSURE: full sun
SOIL: well drained

In the North, use as an annual. In the South, it blooms year-round but can become invasive; plant in containers or use barriers in the soil. The shrubby forms can be used for background planting or can be trained on a wall, trellis, or fence. Pruned to uniform height, it can be planted in mixed flower beds. The dwarf, spreading varieties can be used as ground cover or can be trimmed to make a foreground edging plant. Additional species: *L. montevidensis* (trailing lantana), plus named hybrids that are a cross between *L. camara* and *L. montevidensis*. These hybrids offer many colors and forms.

Lavandula angustifolia   (lavender, English lavender)
Family Lamiaceae   (mint)

TYPE: small shrub
HEIGHT: 1 to 3 feet
FLOWER COLOR: lavender, purple

BLOOM SEASON: summer
EXPOSURE: full sun
SOIL: well drained, alkaline

Can be used as foreground or edging plant or in mixed perennial garden. Fragrant. Requires cutting back annually. Additional species: *L. dentata* (French lavender).

Liatris spicata   (spike gayfeather, spike blazing-star)
Family Asteraceae   (sunflower or composite)

TYPE: hardy perennial
HEIGHT: 2 to 3 feet
FLOWER COLOR: pinkish purple to lavender

BLOOM SEASON: midsummer to fall
EXPOSURE: full sun
SOIL: tolerates poor soil

Plant singly or in a mass. Flower plumes grow to 15 inches. Good cut flower. Additional species: *L. pycnostachya* (Kansas gayfeather); *L. scariosa* (tall gayfeather).

Ligustrum japonicum   (wax-leaf privet, Japanese privet)
Family Oleaceae   (olive)

TYPE: evergreen shrub
HEIGHT: 6 to 18 feet, depending on pruning
FLOWER COLOR: creamy white

BLOOM SEASON: summer to early fall
EXPOSURE: full sun to shade
SOIL: tolerates wide range of soils

Dark green, lustrous foliage. Pruned, this is a common hedge plant. Untrimmed, it is suitable for background foundation planting.

Lonicera japonica   (Japanese honeysuckle)
Family Caprifoliaceae (honeysuckle)

TYPE: semievergreen vine
HEIGHT: height depends upon support
FLOWER COLOR: white, rose tint; yellows with age

BLOOM SEASON: late spring to early fall
EXPOSURE: full sun, light shade
SOIL: tolerates poor soil

Semievergreen in South, deciduous in North; requires light shade in hot climates. Rapidly growing plant; can be trained up a wall, fence, or trellis for background foliage; fragrant flowers. With major pruning, can be used as foreground edging plant. Can be invasive; not recommended where it cannot be strictly controlled.

Mentha spp.   (mints)
Family Lamiaceae   (mint)

TYPE: hardy perennials
HEIGHT: 1 to 4 feet
FLOWER COLOR: lavender and
  white

BLOOM SEASON: summer to fall
EXPOSURE: partial shade
SOIL: moist

Aromatic. Invasive; spread rapidly by underground stems.

Monarda didyma   (bee balm, Oswego tea)
Family Lamiaceae   (mint)

TYPE: hardy perennial
HEIGHT: 2 to 4 feet
FLOWER COLOR: red

BLOOM SEASON: summer to fall
EXPOSURE: full sun, light shade
SOIL: moist, rich

Native to eastern U.S. Taller-growing varieties good in mixed perennial garden. Mint aroma. Additional species: *M. fistulosa* (wild bergamot), rosy lavender, 3 to 4 feet.

Nicotiana alata   (flowering tobacco)
Family Solanaceae   (nightshade)

TYPE: half-hardy perennial
HEIGHT: 2 to 3 feet
FLOWER COLOR: white, red,
  pink

BLOOM SEASON: all summer
EXPOSURE: full sun, light shade
SOIL: well drained

Treat as annual except in warm areas, where it will reseed or winter over. Fragrant.

Petunia × *hybrida*   (common garden petunia)
Family Solanaceae   (nightshade)

TYPE: annual
HEIGHT: 1 foot plus
FLOWER COLOR: wide range,
  including white, purple,
  lavender/blue, red, pink, and
  yellow

BLOOM SEASON: summer to fall
EXPOSURE: full sun
SOIL: good garden soil with
  adequate moisture

Produce very showy, strong, clear-colored flowers; also available in softer shades. Some forms are upright; others cascade over the edge of a planter or wall. Can be used as foreground edging plant, mass-planted, or blended with other plants near the front of a border.

Phlox paniculata   (garden phlox, summer phlox, hardy phlox)
Family Polemoniaceae   (phlox)

TYPE: hardy perennial
HEIGHT: 2 to 4 feet
FLOWER COLOR: white, salmon, scarlet, lilac, purple

BLOOM SEASON: all summer
EXPOSURE: full sun, light shade
SOIL: slightly acid, moist

Can be used in a single mass planting, in one or more colors. Fragrant. Mulch around plant to keep cool and moist. The old-fashioned garden phlox blooms in late summer, but you can select varieties that bloom earlier.

Rosmarinus officinalis   (rosemary)
Family Lamiaceae   (mint)

TYPE: small shrub
HEIGHT: 2 to 6 feet
FLOWER COLOR: pale blue

BLOOM SEASON: early spring; winter in warmer climates
EXPOSURE: full sun
SOIL: well drained

Fragrant culinary herb. Gray-green foliage. Dwarf varieties useful as foreground edging plant. Taller varieties can be pruned as hedge.

Rudbeckia spp.   (black-eyed Susan, coneflowers)
Family Asteraceae   (sunflower or composite)

TYPE: hardy perennial
HEIGHT: 2½ to 3½ feet
FLOWER COLOR: golden yellow with dark eye in center

BLOOM SEASON: midsummer to early fall
EXPOSURE: full sun
SOIL: well drained

Can be mass-planted in one uniform planting or in mixed perennial bed. Good cut flower. Plant in light shade in hot climates. Common species: *R. hirta* (black-eyed Susan, a cultivated variety of this species, is called gloriosa daisy) and *R. fulgida* (orange coneflower). *R. fulgida* 'Goldsturm' (2 feet) is an excellent cultivar and is widely available.

Scabiosa caucasica   (pincushion flower)
Family Dipsacaceae   (teasel)

TYPE: biennial and hardy perennial
HEIGHT: 1½ to 2½ feet
FLOWER COLOR: light blue, white

BLOOM SEASON: midsummer through early fall
EXPOSURE: full sun
SOIL: moist, well drained

Good in mixed or massed plantings. Good dried or cut flower. Prefers mild climates; plant in light shade in hot climates.

Sedum spectabile   (showy stonecrop)
Family Crassulaceae   (orpine)

TYPE: annual
HEIGHT: 18 to 24 inches
FLOWER COLOR: pink to rosy red

BLOOM SEASON: late summer to late fall
EXPOSURE: full sun, light shade
SOIL: well drained

Can be used as edging plant or in mixed perennial garden. Succulentlike, grayish green foliage; tight flower-bud clusters. Flowers turn bronze color by early fall. Flowers dry on the plant and provide color all winter. Many cultivars are widely available and allow precise flower color selection. *S. spectabile* 'Autumn Joy' is an outstanding plant and an example of the fine cultivars.

Solidago spp.   (goldenrods)
Family Asteraceae   (sunflower or composite)

TYPE: hardy perennials
HEIGHT: 1 to 3 feet
FLOWER COLOR: golden yellow

BLOOM SEASON: late summer to early fall
EXPOSURE: full sun
SOIL: well drained

Good in mixed or massed plantings. Good cut flower.

Tagetes patula **(French marigold)**
Family Asteraceae   (sunflower or composite)

TYPE: annual

HEIGHT: 6 to 18 inches

FLOWER COLOR: various golds
with dark red markings

BLOOM SEASON: early summer
to fall

EXPOSURE: full sun

SOIL: well drained

The small, compact varieties are colorful and good for foreground edging. Good cut flower.

Zinnia elegans **(common zinnia)**
Family Asteraceae   (sunflower or composite)

TYPE: annual

HEIGHT: 1 to 3 feet

FLOWER COLOR: wide variety

BLOOM SEASON: midsummer to
fall

EXPOSURE: full sun

SOIL: well drained

Brilliantly colored plants with a wide selection of both color and size; work well in mixed or massed planting. Dwarf forms can be used as foreground edging plant. Good cut flower.

The common spring moth (*Heliomata cycladata*) nectaring at dame's rocket (*Hesperis matronalis*). Lines of bright, metallic scales festoon its wings, Arnot Forest, Ithaca, New York.
JIM MESSINA, PRAIRIE WINGS

Moths and the Garden at Night

Dave Winter

T HE GARDEN DOES NOT go to sleep at night. As the light fades, butterflies select their roosting spots amid tall grass or beneath broad leaves, and moths begin to take their places. They have been resting during the day, camouflaged on tree trunks or twigs, hidden in crevices or within the leaf litter. They first appear at dusk, different species choosing different depths of darkness, different times in the night to emerge. Most of them pass unnoticed: how many gardeners prowl about in the dark, inspecting blossoms by flashlight?

There are more than ten thousand species of moths in North America, fourteen times the number of butterfly species. Yet compared with butterflies, moths are looked upon as second-class citizens. If they receive any press coverage, it is usually derogatory. Despite their reputation for destruction, however, the larvae of less than one-tenth of 1 percent of moth species threaten your woolens. The larvae of many moths are serious agricultural pests, but they are also the primary food of large numbers of our songbirds, particularly when the birds are rearing their young.

Why are some of us so attracted, so addicted, to moths? Perhaps it is because they may be likened to some people who seem dull at first sight, but on further acquaintance turn out to be unexpectedly interesting or flamboyant or downright fascinating. Indeed, some moths remain forever dull. But many, with their intricate markings, their cryptic camouflage patterning and posturing, their subtle pastel coloring, or their unexpected flashing brilliance (often concealed when the moth is at rest), are worthy rivals of the most showy butterfly. Variety provides an additional lure. Within a few years a butterfly watcher will become acquainted with all the species frequenting a given area. It is doubtful that a moth observer can accomplish this feat in a lifetime. There are always more moths to discover.

Moths patronize a garden for the same reasons butterflies do. They are primarily seeking nectar from blossoms to serve as fuel for flight and reproduction. They may also sample other incidental attractions—extracting fluid from animal feces or from the carcass of a toad that ignored the mower, sipping sap from a broken twig or dying elm (a sap run), drinking juices from fallen fruit. Butterflies favor these offerings also. The neater the garden, the fewer the opportunities.

Moths commonly patronize the same flowers butterflies visit during the day. The milkweeds, garden phlox, dame's rocket, flowering tobacco, dogbane, and many horticultural varieties of composites that do not suffer from too much petal doubling or loss of fragrance are just a few of the flowers attractive to moths. In addition, pussy willows are attractive to sallow and pinion moths. These moths are distinguished largely by their drabness; some hibernate, and some emerge from their pupae on the first warm days of spring. When the willow catkins turn yellow, these small moths turn from sap runs to willow blossoms for nourishment.

Whether moths choose flowers on the basis of fragrance, color, or form is not yet clearly understood. An argument for fragrance is that moths are strongly attracted to sap runs that are sugary or fermented and to the juices of overripe or rotting fruit. These have no particular form or color and are readily located on the darkest night. To the human nose, the fragrance of many of the attractive flowers seems greater in the evening and at night. If this apparently increased fragrance is not merely a result of higher humidity and diminished air movement, then it is another argument for odor. On the other hand, studies of the wildflower scarlet gilia indicate that a sphinx moth, the white-lined sphinx, prefers to nectar at pale pink rather than more deeply colored blossoms. And arguments can be made for form: large moths with very long tongues visit flowers with long, tubular throats which other insects cannot exploit.

While the flower is serving the moth its nourishment, the moth is serving the flower as well. Moths captured while nectaring at flowers, or after, commonly have pollen grains adhering to the tongue, the scales of the head and thorax, and the legs. Nectar-feeding moths are major pollinators, less important than bees to most flowers but absolutely essential to some species. The yucca moths—and they alone—must pollinate the yucca so the plant can produce its seeds, which the moth depends on for its larval food. The common evening primrose is capable of self-pollination. But

The white-lined sphinx (*Hyles lineata*) at flowering tobacco (*Nicotiana alata*).
This moth may be seen hovering at flowers at dawn, at dusk, in bright sunlight,
and also at night. It ranges through most of North America.
JIM MESSINA, PRAIRIE WINGS

cross-pollination is performed by the primrose moth, whose larvae feed on
the developing seed pods of the primrose. And certain tropical flowers
have tubular throats so long they are capable of being pollinated only by
sphinx moths with tongues equally long—in some species more than ten
inches.

Observing moths in the garden at dusk and at dawn is little different
from watching butterflies—the existing light is sufficient for spotting the
moth and studying its behavior. The aspect and behavior of the moth,
however, are generally less flamboyant than those of the butterfly. Colors
are mostly subdued and are, in addition, made less apparent by a whirring,
rather than a fluttering, action of the wings. Most moths hover, like a hummingbird, while taking nectar. Some settle down and walk about unobtru-
sively over the flower head.

When darkness deepens, artificial light becomes a necessity. This is not
to say that the garden should be illuminated with floodlights. To do so

would only distract the moths from their business and draw them toward the lights. Female moths are less readily attracted to light and would probably ignore the illuminated area.

A flashlight is a better answer, but drawbacks remain. If it is bright, the light may draw the moth away from its nectaring or frighten it away. A flashlight subdued with a filter of yellow or red plastic film, or even a

Yucca moths (*Tegeticula yuccasella*) resting within a yucca blossom (*Yucca filamentosa*). The yucca depends on this moth for pollination, and the moth larvae feed on its developing seeds.   JOHN M. COFFMAN

The hummingbird moth (*Hemaris thysbe*) at wild bergamot (*Monarda fistulosa*). A day-flying sphinx moth, it is frequently seen hovering and sipping nectar at deep-throated blossoms. PETER W. POST

yellow paper napkin, is less disturbing. A pinhead-sized coppery glint from the hovering insect's compound eye may be the first clue to its presence. Step a little closer and the blur of its wings and the outline of its cylindrical body become apparent as it dips its long, uncoiled tongue into one floret after another. Following its quick moves from one flower head to another can be a real challenge.

Moonlight is not an answer for nighttime moth watching. Fewer moths are attracted to lights and to sap runs on clear, moonlit nights. It is not certain whether fewer moths are on the wing at such times, or whether changes in the moths' behavior make observation more difficult.

Many, but not all, families of moths visit flowers for nectar. Most obvious and most massive of the nectar-feeders are the sphinx moths, or hawkmoths. These names are somewhat inappropriate. It is the larvae of the sphinx moths that rest in a posture suggesting that of the Sphinx, and the moths are certainly not raptors or predators. The avian behavior they emulate is that of the hummingbird, which some of the hawkmoths exceed in size! Regardless of name, when these lepidopteran behemoths hover and dart among the flowers, they create a fascination in the moth watcher that even hungry mosquitoes cannot dispel. A few species of sphinx moths are observed only rarely, because their preferred feeding time is at the crack of dawn, when few people are out inspecting their gardens.

The noctuid moths are a major group of flower and sweet feeders. A few subgroups are the cutworm moths, the underwing moths, the plusiine looper·moths, and the great black witch. The cutworm moths are small to medium sized, heavy bodied, mostly very drab; they usually hover while feeding. Plusiines are similar in build and behavior but are distinguished by silvery marks on the forewings or in the most striking of all, *Diachrysia balluca*, by a brassy green sheen flashing from the entire forewing.

The underwings are medium-large moths with black hindwings dramatically banded with red, orange, or yellow. They start to appear about two and a half months after leaf buds open on the trees they use for larval food: aspens and willows, oaks, hickories, hawthorns, and others. A sequence of species can be seen from early summer to early fall, but only occasionally on flowers.

A simple recipe can help you detect the presence of underwings in your garden. They are addicted to sweets. Mix together a pound of dark brown sugar and a can of beer; stir in a mashed banana, the more overripe the better. Add a pinch of yeast. Cover the jar, to discourage fruit flies (not tightly, or it may explode), and set it aside in a warm place to work for a few days. Then, at dusk, paint patches of tree trunks or fence posts with the fragrant, sticky mess. Half an hour later, using a subdued flashlight, start revisiting the spots. The sight of a feeding underwing, eyes gleaming and colorful hindwing bands blazing forth in the light, is a match for the most glamorous butterfly seen at high noon.

The geometrid moths, whose larvae are the familiar inchworms, are dainty medium- and small-sized moths with a build similar to butterflies. They are frequently seen fluttering about blossoms or stepping slowly over a flower head, sampling as they go.

While butterflies are rarely active at night (and then generally in response to artificial light), some moths are occasionally seen in broad daylight, and others are regularly active then. An underwing will, now and then, feed at flowers in full sunlight, as will some of the smaller noctuids. Geometrids are often active by day. Many of the diminutive and strikingly

The sweetheart (*Catocala amatrix*), an underwing moth, feeding at a sugar-baited tree trunk. Resting by day on the bark of a tree, its colorful hindwings covered, it can be almost invisible. DON RIEPE, NATIONAL PARK SERVICE

patterned flower moths can be seen buzzing about composite flowers or resting on the discs, where their patterns make them difficult to spot. The pink-and-buff primrose moth, resting within the contrasting yellow blossom of the primrose, is a particularly beautiful treat.

The most familiar daytime visitor, however, is the hummingbird sphinx moth, hovering on transparent wings which compete in form and function with those of its avian model. This species, and its close relatives, can be encouraged in the garden by plantings of *Viburnum*, snowberry, and blueberry, all larval food plants. If squash is being grown nearby, the squash-vine borer moth may be sighted. It also has transparent wings, and it mimics a wasp. But its manner of hovering and the hum of its wings

Luna moth (*Actias luna*). This spectacular moth does not visit flowers but is often attracted at night to lighted windows and porches.   W. B. WALDEN

have a gentler aspect; the antennae look a bit large for a wasp, and the waist is less pinched. Moths easily outstrip butterflies in variety of design.

Many people are familiar with the great silkmoths, which visit their porch lights and window screens. But drawings of these moths feeding— the pale green, long-tailed luna moth, the red-banded cecropia, or the brown polyphemus with its eyelike "shiners"—are artistic license gone awry. When moths of this group end the larval stage, the digestive tract disintegrates and is never rebuilt. The adult moth has no mouthparts and no intestinal tract: it cannot feed. It functions throughout the remainder of its week-long life span on energy stored while it was a larva. Its interest in the garden is limited to selecting the proper shrubs and trees on which to lay its eggs, plants on which its larvae can thrive. These food plants vary from species to species and from one part of the continent to another.

The enjoyment of moths in the garden is fleeting, so it is natural to turn to the camera to record their nighttime activity. A flash is a necessity, and a metered flash is a great convenience. You can obtain greater accuracy if the camera has aperture priority programming, which allows controlled exposure through a smaller aperture and greater depth of focus. But the necessary use of a dim flashlight for critical focusing requires care in order to avoid disturbing the subject. With practice you can obtain very satisfactory photographs, particularly of the underwing moths.

Specific identification of moths as they feed in the garden is not easy. As already indicated, particular groups have their own characteristics and can be readily recognized. Individuals that perch while feeding can be inspected somewhat at leisure. But those that feed while hovering can usually only be guessed at. Which sphinx? Which noctuid? The workable approach may strike some as too cumbersome or seem distasteful to others. The moth must be temporarily captured.

The use of an insect net to sweep the moth off the flower is the easy way. And it is sometimes possible to entrap the moth in a glass jar held in one hand and the cap in the other. If you net the moth, you should transfer it to a covered glass jar which is clean, absolutely dry, and empty; no ventilation holes are necessary. You then place the jar in the refrigerator (not the freezer) until the moth is thoroughly chilled and quiescent, perhaps half an hour or more; then you can identify the moth by comparing it with field-guide illustrations. Once you identify it, allow the moth to warm up and depart—if it has not already done so!

Gardeners who wish to become thoroughly familiar with the moths who share their gardens will need to make a permanent collection—a synoptic collection—which involves killing, spreading, and retaining one or two specimens of each species encountered. Rearing caterpillars to maturity is an additional way to learn about resident moths and butterflies and is a fascinating pursuit in itself. The techniques for making and preserving a small permanent collection are easily learned, as are the procedures for rearing caterpillars successfully. These are outlined succinctly in *A Field Guide to the Butterflies of North America, East of the Great Plains*, by Alexander B. Klots (Boston: Houghton Mifflin, 1951), in *A Field Guide to the Moths of North America*, by Charles V. Covell (Boston: Houghton Mifflin, 1984), and in greater detail in *Butterflies and Moths: A Companion to Your Field Guide*, by Jo Brewer and Dave Winter (Englewood Cliffs, N.J.: Prentice-Hall, 1986).

Limited collection of the species enjoying the average garden (as opposed to those species requiring highly specialized, restricted habitats) is not detrimental to the survival of the species. The collector will remove fewer individuals in a lifetime than a catbird will consume in one nesting season. A moth or butterfly, once it lays its eggs, has no further interest or responsibility in the welfare of its offspring. The Lepidopterists' Society has developed guidelines for reasonable and conservative collecting of moths and butterflies, which are available from the society and are also reprinted in *Butterflies and Moths*.

Finally, moth watchers should be warned about use of a popular device, the ultraviolet-illuminated "bug zapper," which lures night-flying in-

The reversed haploa (*Haploa reversa*), a night-flying moth, usually rests by day beneath a broad leaf. It is occasionally discovered, exposed, in the garden by day.
JIM MESSINA, PRAIRIE WINGS

sects to electrical incineration against a highly charged wire grid. Bug zap-
pers make no major impression on the local mosquito population that they
are intended to control. The killed mosquitoes are continually being replaced by others teeming in from the periphery. They do, however, attract
and destroy many of the larger moths. Nighttime mosquito control is
more effectively accomplished by application of an N,N-diethyl-meta-
toluamide repellent to exposed skin.

Gardeners have broadened their interests from flowers and plants to
include birds and, more recently, butterflies. The next step is for us to open
our eyes to the largely hidden world of moths—their intricacy, their secrecy, and their unexpected beauty.

Female great purple hairstreak (*Atlides halesus*) taking nectar from fogfruit (*Phyla lanceolata*).
JOHN R. RIGGENBACH

Butterfly Gardening and Conservation

~

Stanwyn G. Shetler

T HE GENTLE ART AND PLEASURE of gardening for butterflies is one way to light a slender candle of hope as the relentless forces of humanity disturb, fragment, homogenize, and destroy the natural habitat, snuffing out the shining lights of individual species one by one.

The butterfly garden is a wonderful window on the local environment. Like a light trap for moths or a bird feeder, a butterfly garden lets you know what is in the territory or which way the ecological currents are blowing. It is a telling index of the character and well-being of the neighboring patches of nature.

Every time a butterfly flits about, feeding on the nectar of flowers, or a caterpillar chews a swath through green leaves, it tells the story of animals and plants coevolving. The mere presence of the butterfly species indicates the existence of host-plant species, sometimes quite particular ones, and a natural chain of ecological relationships, including birds and other predators. Butterflies signal a set of evolved interactions, and wherever they fly

Stanwyn G. Shetler is a curator of botany at the National Museum of Natural History, Smithsonian Institution. Since 1984 he has served as an assistant director and the acting deputy director of the museum. Shetler has written more than a hundred scientific, technical, and popular titles, including three books. A lifelong birder, he has served several terms on the board of directors and three years as president of the independent Audubon Naturalist Society of the Central Atlantic States. He has been active in a variety of conservation and environmental causes, among them the national effort to draft biodiversity legislation.

Silver-spotted skipper (*Epargyreus clarus*) on dogbane (*Apocynum cannabinum*), Rockingham County, Virginia.   JOHN M. COFFMAN

they make a living statement about the vitality of their own natural environment.

But one butterfly or one wildflower does not an ecosystem make. Nature's rich complement of butterflies and flowers and other organisms and their myriad, evolved relationships can only survive if the diversity of the natural habitat is preserved.

The natural landscape is a patchwork of diverse habitats, organisms, and relationships. This patchwork has many layers of interrelated histories—geological, environmental, evolutionary, and ecological—and is a dynamic expression of the current health of the natural estate. It includes histories of migrations, dispersals, invasions, human disturbances, extinctions, and many other events. It is the culmination of a long stream of evolutionary history. The extinction of a species measurably diminishes the spectrum of biological diversity in the habitat and destroys a strand of history.

Virtually all landscapes have been compromised by human disturbance, virtually all natural histories garbled by human histories. This is the inevitable consequence of human existence. The conservation challenge to present-day keepers of the land is to understand that the natural estate cradles, binds together, and adorns the man-made estate, but that the man-made estate can overwhelm or destroy the natural estate. The ultimate goal is to preserve the integrity of both realms and, above all, to let the natural realm continue to tell its own original story in as unadulterated a state as possible.

A natural ecosystem is more than the sum of its parts, especially in its historical continuity, and it cannot be concocted like a cake from a mix of ingredients. Sowing, transplanting, or releasing plant and animal species indiscriminately across the land is neither sufficient nor necessarily wise as a conservation strategy. The urge to play Johnny Appleseed must be resisted, or else the world will become a zoo or botanical garden without a traceable history and the biota will be homogenized from coast to coast. Even a "wild" flower is no longer a native but an introduced exotic if it is purposely planted in the wild.

Surely the most compelling reason for butterfly gardening is to increase public awareness of the critical importance of saving butterflies and other animals and plants by saving their natural habitats. In this context, gardening is a means of preservation, rehabilitation, and restoration. By cultivating plants for butterflies, gardeners will increase their awareness of nature and of the precarious state of the natural environment, and recognize the necessity of preserving as much of the natural habitat as possible.

Small copper (*Lycaena phlaeas*) on wild strawberry (*Fragaria virginiana*), Virginia.
TOM PIERSON

Wildflowers in the Planned Landscape

~
David K. Northington

A PROPER SELECTION OF native wildflowers can provide gardens
with overlapping seasons of both flower color and visiting butterflies. Wildflowers contribute aesthetically to the landscape and
demonstrate to the gardener a basic principle of conservation: the inter-
dependency of native animals and plants. Animal species, such as butterflies of a particular region, are often specifically coadapted with the native
plants of that region.

Cultivating native species is an important step toward reversing their
destruction. A world population now exceeding five billion requires more
highways, houses, and cities. In the United States alone, some 220 acres
of land are lost each hour to highway and urban development. More land,
much of it marginally arable, is being brought into cultivation.

The loss of native plant communities is a primary cause of species extinction. Of the approximately twenty thousand species of native plants in
North America, about three thousand are at risk of extinction. In addition,
natural plant communities have been reduced and significantly altered by
the introduction of nonnative plants that crowd out native species and rad-

*David K. Northington is executive director of the National Wildflower Research Center
(NWRC), a nonprofit organization that supports the conservation of existing natural populations of indigenous plant species and the fauna they support and depend upon. The NWRC
emphasizes the advantages of planting community groupings of indigenous species—replicat-
ing in gardens the diversity of plant species that occurs naturally in a given area. The library
of the NWRC information clearinghouse serves as a national resource center for information*

Male cloudless sulfur (*Phoebis sennae*) on composite.   JOHN R. RIGGENBACH

ically change the environment that sustains them. Destroying native plant communities also reduces natural erosion control, removes much of the genetic potential from individual plant species, and disturbs the natural resting and feeding habitat of regional fauna.

Taking into consideration all the plants and animals in the world, some biologists estimate there is one plant species for every seven to fifteen animal species. Therefore, the loss of a plant species affects the ecology of a

on what, when, and how to plant, where to find seed and nursery-grown plants, and establishment and management techniques. Much of this information is also available in their publications, which include a full-color book, Wildflowers Across America *(New York: Abbeville Press, 1988), by NWRC founder Lady Bird Johnson, Carlton B. Lees, and Les Line, a 105-page album of the best-loved and most spectacular of America's wildflowers. For information about other publications and membership, write to the NWRC, 2600 FM 973 North, Austin, Texas 78725, or call (512) 929-3600.*

number of animal species. Most plants, in turn, depend upon animals for such ecological services as pollination and seed dispersal. Neither plants nor butterflies can exist alone as independent entities.

It is time to focus on the remaining native wildflowers, grasses, shrubs, and trees, and the animals associated with them, and to protect as much of this natural heritage as possible. Furthermore, native species should be reestablished in the habitat zones to which they are or were indigenous. In the best case, this would mean that new plantings of native species would imitate naturally occurring groups in order to provide active ecological communities for interdependent animals and plants.

The use of propagated plants or seeds is the only suitable way to add to existing flora. Removing wild plants from their natural habitats disturbs those habitats and results in a net loss of plants because only a percentage of transplants survive.

The philosophy of planting natives will only work if species are selected carefully. Introducing a species or variety from outside its natural

Sleepy orange (*Eurema nicippe*) on Arizona or desert poppy (*Kallstroemia grandiflora*), Arizona. EDWARD S. ROSS

range—even from one side of a state to another—is little different from introducing it from another continent. Nonnative species may die, adjust successfully to their new environment, or become competitive and invasive. Only the second possibility is not obviously negative; and even in that case, local plants must share resources that previously were fully available only to them. Moreover, the survival of an introduced species does not necessarily mean that it truly naturalizes, in the sense that it becomes a productive part of the natural ecosystem.

Consideration of the total habitat is essential. Whether planting isolated individuals as part of a formal landscaping plan or planting community groupings in yard or garden, it is the cumulative effect of these plantings that is most important. This is especially true for pollinators whose foraging ranges include separate native populations and landscape plantings. In planning a butterfly garden, include a selection of local native species that provide for the butterfly throughout its life cycle. Although an acre of restored prairie or open woodland is wonderful, smaller, separate

Male tailed orange (*Eurema proterpia*), summer form, on sticky spine-aster (*Machaeranthera bigelovii*), Arizona.   EDWARD S. ROSS

Female two-tailed swallowtail (*Papilio multicaudata*) on cardinal flower (*Lobelia cardinalis*), Sycamore Canyon, Arizona. EDWARD S. ROSS

groups of plant species native to such an area will also provide for the feeding and reproductive needs of butterflies and other pollinators.

Finally, plant species that are truly rare in nature in their own right probably should not be used for butterfly gardening. Butterflies are unlikely to use them.

Within these guidelines, the National Wildflower Research Center (NWRC) encourages everyone who enjoys the beauty of native flowers and butterflies to reestablish native habitat. And while no absolute rules for reestablishing habitat exist, guidelines are available from the NWRC, and they should be studied carefully. Planning, patience, and persistence are the keys to success. The learning process is an exciting adventure, and the end result is certainly worth the effort. The more gardeners add to the interactive communities of butterflies and native plants, the more stable and colorful the world will become.

Larva of green hairstreak (*Callophrys viridis*) on wild buckwheat (*Eriogonum latifolium*), San Bruno Mountain, California.   EDWARD S. ROSS

Enriching Your
Personal Landscape
~
Edward S. Ross

NATIVE PLANTS CAN BE likened to theatrical settings. In its native home each plant species is the backdrop and producer of an age-old drama—one with a well-rehearsed cast of actors, mostly insects. When an exotic plant or even a native but not locally indigenous species is moved to a new land or locale, the cast of actors is left behind, and there is no plot, no play, for an interested audience to witness and enjoy.

In constructing a new home or landscaping an old one, many people strip a site of its native vegetation, its backdrop. They plant broad lawns, which waste space, water, and labor, and which distance them from nature. They replace butterfly-rich indigenous plants with a hodgepodge of exotic plants.

My ideal garden is one rich in biological theater, abounding with butterflies and other creatures dependent on native plants. The home is sited in a natural environment which is intrinsically beautiful and needs little or no improvement or even upkeep. Nature is the groundskeeper.

Edward S. Ross is a pioneer of close-up insect photography. His candid field photography of Lepidoptera and many other subjects is used at all educational levels in a wide range of technical and popular media: television films, film strips, exhibits, booklets, textbooks, trade books, magazines, and children's books and magazines. After receiving degrees in entomology at the University of California, Berkeley, Ross began a fifty-year career as curator of entomology at the California Academy of Sciences in San Francisco. In quest of specimens to serve his research on the insect order Embiidina (web-spinners), he has conducted numerous and extensive ex-

Buckeye (*Junonia coenia*) nectaring at composite, California.   EDWARD S. ROSS

A few paths provide comfortable access and allow close observation of the small dramas that unfold along the way. If the site is too densely wooded, glades and open edges are cleared to let in the sun and increase native plant diversity and the number of butterfly host plants. Insecticides and herbicides are never used, regardless of the severity of a pest outbreak. Watching natural enemies take charge of the problem is part of the garden drama.

In such a paradise you can enjoy season after season of biotic events—the burst of spring, floral sequences, and the lives of interesting creatures.

peditions to all tropical regions. His web-spinner collection, about three hundred thousand specimens, serves as the basis of major monographs describing hundreds of new species. His general collection of insects, totaling perhaps a million specimens, is maintained at the California Academy of Sciences, which loans portions to research specialists all over the world. Ross's photographs appear throughout Butterfly Gardening: Creating Summer Magic in Your Garden *and accompany the following two essays.*

Male gulf fritillary (*Agraulis vanillae*), Sycamore Canyon, Arizona. EDWARD S. ROSS

Disappointments must be expected if your garden is but an oasis in the midst of a frequently sprayed neighborhood far removed from the creek margins, meadows, and woodlands which normally serve as source areas for butterflies. Many butterflies do not fly very far and may not be able to find an isolated table of food and nectar plants especially set for their palates. In such cases, a broad community interest in butterfly gardening, perhaps an adjunct activity of a local garden club, is needed so there will be an extensive build-up of resident butterflies in many adjacent gardens. Perhaps, eventually, these gardens will grow to form a biotic bridge to outlying natural plant communities.

We can maintain contact and harmony with natural environments by treating our immediate surroundings—our personal landscapes—with sensitivity and respect, by supporting the acquisition of open space and wildlife preserves both near and far, and by supporting well-advised stewardship of the natural landscape.

Larva of queen (*Danaus gilippus*) and milkweed bugs on milkweed pod (*Asclepias* sp.), San Pedro, Baja California Sur. EDWARD S. ROSS

Butterfly Photography
~
Edward S. Ross

H AVING A RICH BUTTERFLY haunt at your doorstep gives you
the opportunity to observe and photograph life histories on
the living host plant without using a breeding cage. A garden
with many butterfly nectar sources and caterpillar food plants may also increase your encounters with adult butterflies nectaring at flowers.

To get candid images of butterflies in your garden you must move
slowly and always be prepared to shoot a suddenly encountered subject.
Unpredictable encounters are variable and require quick decisions: Is my
approach unobstructed? Is the background okay? Is my focus sharp? Is the
camera properly set? You always hope that the butterfly will be doing
something of interest—mating, laying eggs, or eating—rather than simply
sitting. At times you must deliberately frighten a subject and hope that it
will alight in a more favorable place. But all too often you never see it
again.

A 35-mm, single-lens reflex camera is basic to candid nature photography. Any of the major brands will do. Ideally, you should use a macro
lens, a lens designed for very short lens-to-subject approaches but useful
for long shots as well. Magnifications are attained by adding one or more
metal extension tubes between the lens and camera body. These should
have internal levers coupling the camera body and lens diaphragm so that
you can focus with the lens wide open and yet expect it to snap to a fine,
preset aperture when the shutter is released.

West Coast lady (*Vanessa annabella*) drinking nectar from a composite,
California.   EDWARD S. ROSS

An electronic flash is vital to most close-up photography—in daylight
as well as at night—because it eliminates one of its most troublesome
problems—variable light. With a flash you have the potential for instant
bursts of intense light. You can vary the light angle and the exposure by
the flash head's distance from the subject. Movement of the subject or photographer is frozen by the speed of light. The light from a flash makes a
fine lens aperture possible, and this results in a great depth of field (that is,
all portions of the subject are likely to be in focus).

To gain these advantages, the flash must be off-camera, not attached
on a "hot shoe," or on brackets. I don't recommend the use of a ring light
because it has a fixed position and direction. My practice is to hold the flash
head in my left hand, usually directed down about ten inches above the
subject, while my right hand operates the camera. I usually preset the lens
to f/22 or f/32 and the shutter at the fastest synchronization speed.

The main disadvantage of flash is that backgrounds beyond the
"throw" of the light will be black, and thus black portions of the subject,

Mormon fritillaries (*Speyeria mormonia*) mating, Ruby Mountains, Nevada.
EDWARD S. ROSS

Full-grown larva of silver-spotted skipper (*Epargyreus clarus*), Water's Creek
State Park, Georgia. EDWARD S. ROSS

such as antennae, will not be visible. You might overcome this problem by inserting a background card or a broad leaf behind the subject, but usually this isn't possible.

Although night photography is impossible without a flash, occasionally, when conditions are right, you can utilize natural light during the day. The greatest advantage is that the background, however distant, can be correctly exposed and appear as pleasant, softly diffused greens and browns.

Natural-light photography has many limitations: the subject must be motionless, the surface plane must be as flat as possible, and you may have to use a tripod for a slow shutter speed and a fine aperture. Using a tripod has its own limitations. Its legs may be too short for above-head shots or too long for ground-level subjects. Also, by the time the tripod is set up, the butterfly may have left the scene. Night photography is impossible without a flash. Of course, you can overcome some available light prob-

Sociable drinkers: male echo blues (*Celastrina argiolus echo*) on mud, Mill Valley, California. EDWARD S. ROSS

Snout butterfly (*Libytheana carinenta*) on cardinal flower (*Lobelia cardinalis*), Sycamore Canyon, Arizona.   EDWARD S. ROSS

lems by using high-speed film, but I do all of my work with slow-speed films of ASA 25 and 64.

Laboratory (or table-top) photography can be an essential adjunct to field efforts. The equipment and its operation are similar to those used in the field. The major difference is that the subjects—eggs, caterpillars, pupae, and adults—are under the control of the photographer, thereby allowing many variations in technique and background. For very high magnifications, such as that required for eggs, a tripod is a must, and a bellows may be desirable (bellows are too fragile for field use).

There is now a confusing array of complex automatic cameras, lenses, and flash units on the market, but I use none of these and continue to take good photographs with my cheaper, older, manual equipment. You must learn, as I did starting more than thirty years ago, by trial and error. Finally, give close attention to photographs you admire. As in word-writing, you learn much about light-writing—photography—by studying good, published examples to understand why the statements are good and what could have been done to have made them better.

Zebra (*Heliconius charitonius*) taking nectar from lantana (*Lantana camara*).   JOHN R. RIGGENBACH

Butterfly-Watching Tips
~
Robert Michael Pyle

T HE REWARDS OF BUTTERFLY watching are many and its pursuit
is simple. Expenses and equipment needs are few. All you have to
do is find butterflies, clear your mind, really open your eyes, and
literally see what happens. I know of no better place to do it than in a
butterfly garden.

Butterflies are most easily observed when they are engaged in feeding.
Watching them rapidly fly past can be frustrating. But butterflies can become so involved in nectaring that you can approach or even touch them
without putting them to flight.

Getting to know butterflies on a first-name basis gives watching much
of its joy. Although field guides will help you identify butterflies, you need
to learn how to approach them. By observing these insects at close range
you will gain the knowledge that enables you to say with confidence,
"That's a red admiral," or "Here we have a checkered skipper." You will
come to know that swallowtails and fritillaries have a special fondness for

*Xerces Society founder **Robert Michael Pyle** is the author of six books on butterflies, including*
The Audubon Society Handbook for Butterfly Watchers *(New York: Charles Scribner's
Sons, 1984), for which he won a Governor's Writers Award in 1985. His latest book,* Win-
tergreen: Listening to the Land's Heart *(Boston: Houghton Mifflin, 1987), describes the
destructive effects of logging on the Willapa Hills of southwest Washington State.* Winter-
green *won the prestigious John Burroughs Medal for distinguished nature writing. After
earning a doctorate in ecology and environmental studies from Yale University, Pyle worked
for several conservation organizations. He is now a full-time writer of essays and fiction.*

Male cloudless sulfur (*Phoebis sennae*) taking nectar from coral bean or cardinal-spear (*Erythrina herbacea*).   JOHN R. RIGGENBACH

thistle and mint nectar, while hairstreaks love dogbane and milkweed. Crescent-spots flap and glide, but skippers, of similar color and size, fly with quick, jerky movements. Soon, basic discrimination is easy, and you become a sharper observer in the process of having fun.

Watching butterflies can make you something of a field botanist. A special pleasure develops in finding or providing a patch of a plant that you know harbors a certain butterfly, then returning to that clump at the right time of year, and presto!—the butterfly is there, on schedule.

Sharp eyes are essential. A butterfly net can be handy, providing a good look at the stronger, more powerful fliers that seldom land. With a net, a whole group can have a close look at a butterfly that might otherwise be disturbed by numbers of people. A little practice perfects usage of a net. It is critical to follow through so that the target insect is swept deep into the net bag. If you are gentle and use care, you can examine butterflies and then release them without harm.

A good pair of tweezers, such as those sold in stamp shops, is the most useful piece of equipment. Experienced butterfly watchers can pluck a butterfly from a flower head, examine it closely, and then return it to its perch none the worse for wear.

A hand lens, preferably 10×, reveals the wonders of butterfly structure: the facets of the eye, the fur of the face, the scales of the wings, the

Female common checkered skipper (*Pyrgus communis*) sipping nectar from a composite, Douglas County, Nebraska. JOHN WEBER, JR.

Mourning cloak (*Nymphalis antiopa*), California.   EDWARD S. ROSS

iridescent hairs of the body, the coiled proboscis (which can gently be pulled out to its full length with a grass stalk). If you are careful, you can use a hand lens to watch a nectaring butterfly up close, without dislodging it. Binoculars are almost as helpful to the butterfly watcher as to the birder. Binoculars enable you to spot butterflies in trees, to follow their flight, and to observe those too wary for close approach. Lower-powered binoculars that focus closer than most are best for butterflies. Opera glasses work, but the ideal is one of the compact 6× models.

A notebook and pencil are essential. In your watching you will surely see things worth remembering, and these should be recorded along with the date and precise location. Detailed behavioral observations, such as territorial, courtship, and predator encounters, are certainly worth recording. Spot a butterfly taking shelter in a storm or at dusk? Write it down. The occurrence of a species in a given area is valuable information that can help you develop a distributional picture of your region.

When observing butterflies, remember to move slowly and fluidly. Rapid movements put butterflies to flight. Unlike birds, butterflies will not necessarily fly away from the flash of bright clothing. Regarding colors as potential mates, competitors, or flowers, butterflies may investigate and even alight on your hat or shirt. Bright bandanas may serve as bait to bring coy butterflies closer.

Sun-basking butterflies seek to warm their blood and flight muscles, affording you the opportunity to view their full-spread wings. Butterfly activity tends to be restricted to warm daylight hours. Because butterflies are cold-blooded and cannot fly without thermal heating from the sun, many species disappear from sight when clouds block the sun. This does not rule out butterfly watching in cloudy weather. With practice you can find butterflies and caterpillars where they take shelter.

Some butterflies emerge as adults from their chrysalids early in the spring, and others do so late into autumn. Mourning cloaks and their relatives overwinter as adults and may even be seen flying on sunny midwinter days. Butterflies fly virtually year-round in the South. A New England butterfly garden in January offers no guarantee of sightings; but at least it offers the prospect of one, in a season when the sight of one live butterfly can do as much for the spirit as a meadowful in summer.

Zebra (*Heliconius charitonius*) on poinsettia (*Euphorbia pulcherrima*). JOHN R. RIGGENBACH

Afterword
~
Robert Michael Pyle

MAKING A GARDEN FOR butterflies offers the opportunity to join in one of life's unsung yet exquisite pleasures. In creating a special place for butterflies in your life, you not only ensure days of delight and hours of tranquility in exchange for your labor, but you also make a positive contribution toward the conservation of beneficial invertebrates. For every person building diversity in Earth's garden, a thousand are working, often unknowingly, to demolish diversity.

Many might ask, Aren't insects chiefly pests? Surely they are the last things you want to invite into your yard! The arguments for conserving insects and other invertebrates are abundant: they represent more than nine-tenths of life on Earth; they support, along with plants, all the major food chains. They do more to control potential pests than a thousand chemical companies, and a very small proportion of insect species are actually pests.

For anyone willing to watch, butterflies offer a permanent passport away from boredom. The beauty of a swallowtail-studded patch of phlox confers a deep sense of pleasure that flowers alone are unable to match. In the end, the butterflies speak for themselves.

I am very concerned about what I call the *extinction of experience*—the loss of everyday species within our own radius of reach. When we lose the common wildlife in our immediate surroundings, we run the risk of becoming inured to nature's absence, blind to delight, and, eventually, alienated from the land. This is where butterfly gardeners come in—they create

Female orange sulfur (*Colias eurytheme*) sipping nectar from red clover (*Trifolium pratense*), Hubbard County, Minnesota.   JOHN WEBER, JR.

and maintain diverse habitats for species that need not become endangered, bolster the numbers of species in our midst, and collectively engage themselves in the rewarding nearness of nature.

By getting your hands dirty in your chemical-free butterfly garden, you make an actual difference. You create the conditions for invertebrate abundance and diversity instead of destroying them. You, the butterfly gardener, are part of the solution. Imagine!—on every square yard you give to the purpose, you can save thousands and thousands of invertebrates, generation after generation. The butterflies are the most obvious reward; and for every butterfly fluttering about in your garden, you're giving much more back to life.

APPENDICES

Roosting question mark (*Polygonia interrogationis*) on foxtail (*Setaria* sp.).
ALAN K. CHARNLEY

APPENDICES A AND B are a collection of observations and opinions regarding plants used for food by butterflies and moths. Appendix A, a listing of nectar plants, is based on the results of a Xerces Society survey of lepidopterists, botanists, and butterfly gardeners which was compiled and edited by Dr. Paul A. Opler, vice president of the Xerces Society. Appendix B, written by Dr. Opler, lists familiar butterflies and their larval plants. The appendices also provide information on plants included in the "Butterfly Garden Design" chapter. The appendices are not intended to be definitive. The absence of a plant on these lists does not exclude the possibility of its being used by butterflies or moths, nor does its presence guarantee that it will attract them to your garden.

APPENDIX A:
Nectar Plants for North American Butterflies and Moths
~

THE FOLLOWING LIST of nectar plants is organized alphabetically by plant family name. Plants related by family are organized by genus and species. The common name of each plant is given in parentheses (we have attempted to use the most current and widely used names, and for some species we include more than one common name). The list follows these conventions:

* Indicates a horticultural species which grows exclusively or principally in cultivation.

sp. Indicates that the genus is known but the species is uncertain.

spp. Indicates that two or more species of this genus are known to attract butterflies or moths. Usually it can be taken to mean that various species in the genus might potentially attract butterflies or moths.

moths also/moths only Indicates plants which attract moths. If an entry does not include one of these designations, that plant attracts butterflies only.

1–7 Identify the geographic regions in which the plants may be useful as butterfly-gardening plants. (See "Key to Geographical Regions," following.) The indicated regions represent only those for which we have specific recommendations from our consultants. No attempt was made to list all possible regions in which the plant occurs or is useful as a butterfly-attracting plant; note also that the plant may not grow in the wild in all regions listed or throughout a given region.

all regions Indicates that species grows in the wild or under cultivation in all regions but may not be native or naturalized in some or all of them.

MPL Indicates a related entry in the Master Plant List within the text.

Key to Geographical Regions

1 Oregon, Washington, southern British Columbia

2 Arizona, California, Nevada

3 Colorado, Idaho, Montana, Utah, Wyoming, southern Alberta, southern Saskatchewan, southwest Manitoba

4 New Mexico, Texas

5 Illinois, Iowa, Kansas, Minnesota, Missouri, Nebraska, North Dakota, Oklahoma, South Dakota, Wisconsin, southeast Manitoba

6 Alabama, Arkansas, Florida, Georgia, Kentucky, Louisiana, Mississippi, North Carolina, South Carolina, Tennessee, Virginia

7 Connecticut, Delaware, Indiana, Maine, Maryland, Massachusetts, Michigan, New Hampshire, New Jersey, New York, Ohio, Pennsylvania, Rhode Island, Vermont, Washington, D.C., West Virginia, southern Ontario, southern Quebec

Acanthaceae
Ruellia spp. (ruellias, wild petunias), 4

Amaranthaceae
Gomphrena globosa (globe amaranth), 2

Anacardiaceae
Rhus aromatica (fragrant sumac), 4, 7
Rhus glabra (smooth sumac), 5, 7
Rhus trilobata (squawbush), 2–5
Rhus typhina (staghorn sumac), 6, 7
*Schinus terebinthifolius (Brazilian peppertree), 4

Apocynaceae
Apocynum androsaemifolium (spreading dogbane), all regions
Apocynum cannabinum (Indian hemp), all regions
*Nerium oleander (oleander), moths only, 4
Trachelospermum difforme (climbing dogbane), moths only, 4

Asclepiadaceae
*Araujia sericifera (bladder flower), 2, 4
Asclepias cordifolia (western purple
    milkweed), 2
Asclepias curassavica (bloodflower), 2, 4
Asclepias eriocarpa (milkweed), 2
Asclepias fascicularis (narrowleaf milkweed), 2
Asclepias incarnata (swamp milkweed), 4–7   *MPL*
Asclepias speciosa (showy milkweed), 1–3, 5
Asclepias syriaca (common milkweed), 5–7
Asclepias tuberosa (butterfly weed, orange milkweed), 3–7   *MPL*
Asclepias verticillata (whorled milkweed), 3, 4
Asclepias spp. (milkweeds), all regions
Cynanchum laeve (honeyvine, sandvine), 4
Sarcostemma cynanchoides (climbing milkweed), 4

Asteraceae, also Compositae
Achillea millefolium (common yarrow, milfoil), 1–3, 6, 7   *MPL*
*Ageratum houstonianum (ageratum, flossflower), all regions
Anaphalis margaritacea (pearly everlasting), 1
Antennaria neglecta (field pussytoes), 5, 7
Aster chilensis (western common aster), 2

Aster ericoides (heath or many-flowered aster), 2, 5, 7

Aster lateriflorus (calico aster), 2, 7

Aster novae-angliae (New England aster), 5   *MPL*

Aster novi-belgii (New York aster), all regions   *MPL*

Aster patens (late purple or spreading aster), 2, 7

Aster porteri (Porter's aster), 3

*Aster × frikartii (Frikart aster), all regions   *MPL*

Aster spp. (asters), all regions

Baccharis glutinosa (sticky baccharis, seep willow), 4

Baccharis pilularis (dwarf baccharis, coyotebrush), 2

Bidens pilosa (shepherd's-needle), 4, 6

Bidens tripartita (European or trifid beggar-ticks), 6, 7

Centaurea spp. (knapweeds, star-thistles, bachelor's-button, or corn-flower), 5, 7

Chrysanthemum leucanthemum (ox-eye daisy), 2, 3, 5–7   *MPL*

*Chrysanthemum maximum (Shasta daisy), all regions   *MPL*

*Chrysanthemum × superbum (Shasta daisy), all regions   *MPL*

Chrysothamnus nauseosus (common or gray rabbit-brush), moths also, 1–5

Chrysothamnus viscidiflorus (green rabbit-brush), moths also, 2–4

Cirsium spp. (thistles), all regions

*Coreopsis grandiflora (large-flowered coreopsis or tickseed), all regions

Coreopsis lanceolata (lance-leaf coreopsis or tickseed), 4, 5

*Coreopsis verticillata (whorled coreopsis or tickseed), all regions

*Cosmos bipinnatus (cosmos), 3–7   *MPL*

Echinacea angustifolia (black-sampson, purple coneflower), 4–7

Echinacea purpurea (purple coneflower), 4, 5, 7   *MPL*

Erigeron spp. (fleabanes), all regions

Eupatorium coelestinum (hardy ageratum, mistflower), 4, 6, 7   *MPL*

Eupatorium fistulosum (hollow Joe-Pye-weed or trumpetweed), 5–7   *MPL*

Eupatorium maculatum (spotted Joe-Pye-weed, smokeweed), 4–7   *MPL*

Eupatorium perfoliatum (common boneset), 4–7

Eupatorium purpureum (sweet or green-stemmed Joe-Pye-weed), 5–7   *MPL*

Eupatorium rugosum (white snakeroot), 6

Gaillardia pulchella (firewheel, Indian-blanket), 4, 5

*Gazania spp. (treasure-flowers), 2

Grindelia spp. (gumweeds), 2–5

Haplopappus arborescens (golden-fleece), 2

Helenium autumnale (sneezeweed), all regions
Helianthus spp. (sunflowers), 2–7   *MPL*
Heliopsis helianthoides (oxeye), 5, 7
Heterotheca villosa (hairy golden-aster), 3
Hieracium spp. (hawkweeds), 6, 7
Hymenopappus filifolius (fineleaf woollywhite), 3
Hymenoxys acaulis (stemless bitterweed or goldflower), 3
Liatris spp. (gayfeathers, blazing-stars), 2–5, 7   *MPL*
Mikania scandens (climbing hempweed), 6
Pluchea purpurascens (salt-marsh fleabane), 2, 7
Ratibida columnifera (Mexican-hat), 3, 5
Rudbeckia fulgida (orange coneflower), all regions   *MPL*
Rudbeckia hirta (black-eyed Susan), 3–7   *MPL*
Rudbeckia laciniata (green-headed coneflower), 3, 4, 7
Senecio douglasii (threadleaf groundsel, creek senecio), 2
Senecio spp. (groundsels, ragworts), 1–5, 7
Solidago graminifolia (grass- or lance-leaved goldenrod), 4
Solidago spp. (goldenrods), all regions   *MPL*
*Tagetes patula (French marigold), all regions   *MPL*
Taraxacum officinale (common dandelion), all regions
Verbesina spp. (crown-beards, wingstem), 4
Vernonia spp. (ironweeds), 5–7
*Zinnia spp. (zinnias), all regions   *MPL*

Balsaminaceae

Impatiens capensis (spotted touch-me-not or jewelweed), 4, 6, 7

Boraginaceae

Amsinckia spp. (fiddlenecks), 2
Cordia boisseri (anacahuita), 4
Cordia spp. (manjacks), 4
Ehretia anacua (anaqua, knackaway), 4
*Heliotropium arborescens (heliotrope, cherry-pie), 2   *MPL*
Lithospermum canescens (hoary puccoon), 4, 5, 7
Myosotis scorpioides (forget-me-not), 7
Symphytum asperum (prickly comfrey), 2, 7
Symphytum officinale (common comfrey), 2, 7

Brassicaceae, also Cruciferae

*Aurinia saxatilis (basket-of-gold), 1
Barbarea vulgaris (winter-cress, yellow-rocket), 6, 7

Brassica spp. (mustards), all regions
Dithyrea wislizenii (spectacle pod), 4
Hesperis matronalis (dame's-rocket), 5, 7
Isatis tinctoria (dyer's woad), 1, 2
Lepidium campestre (field peppergrass), 2
Lepidium latifolium (broad-leaved peppergrass), 2
Lepidium montanum (western peppergrass), 3
*Raphanus sativus (radish), 2, 5, 7
Sisymbrium altissimum (Jim Hill mustard, tumble-mustard), 1, 2
Sisymbrium officinale (hedge-mustard), 1

Cactaceae
Opuntia humifusa (eastern prickly pear), 3–5, 7

Capparaceae
Cleome hasslerana (spider-flower), 3, 4
Cleome serrulata (Rocky Mountain bee-plant), 4, 5

Caprifoliaceae
*Abelia spp. (abelias), 2   *MPL*
Lonicera japonica (Japanese honeysuckle), 4–6   *MPL*
Lonicera spp. (honeysuckles), moths also, all regions
Sambucus spp. (elders, elderberries), 1, 3
Symphoricarpos occidentalis (wolfberry, western snowberry), 3, 5
Symphoricarpos oreophilus (snowberry), 3

Caryophyllaceae
Dianthus armeria (Deptford pink), 6, 7
**Dianthus barbatus* (sweet-William), 7

Clethraceae
Clethra alnifolia (sweet-pepperbush), 4, 6

Convolvulaceae
Convolvulus arvensis (field bindweed), 1, 3–5

Crassulaceae
*Sedum spectabile (showy stonecrop), 2, 5, 7   *MPL*

Dipsacaceae
Dipsacus fullonum (common teasel), all regions
*Scabiosa spp. (pincushions, scabiosas), 2, 7   *MPL*

Ericaceae

Ledum palustre (Labrador-tea), 5, 7

Rhododendron periclymenoides (R. nudiflorum) (pink azalea, pinxter flower), 6, 7

Vaccinium arboreum (farkleberry), 4–6

Vaccinium spp. (blueberries), 5–7

Euphorbiaceae

Euphorbia marginata (snow-on-the-mountain), 2, 7

*Euphorbia pulcherrima (poinsettia), 2

Fabaceae, also Leguminosae

Amorpha canescens (lead-plant), 5–7

Astragalus spp. (milk-vetches), 1–5, 7

Cercis canadensis (redbud), 4–7

Coronilla varia (crown-vetch), 2, 6, 7

Dalea purpurea (purple prairie-clover), 4, 5

Erythrina herbacea (coral bean or cardinal-spear), 4, 6

Hedysarum boreale (northern sweet-vetch), 3

Lathyrus latifolius (everlasting or perennial pea), 1

Lupinus perennis (wild or sundial lupine), 5–7

Medicago sativa (alfalfa), all regions

Melilotus alba (white sweet-clover), all regions

Sophora spp. (sophoras), 4

Trifolium pratense (red clover), all regions

Trifolium repens (white clover), all regions

Vicia americana (American or purple vetch), all regions

Vicia caroliniana (Carolina or wood vetch), all regions

Vicia cracca (cow or tufted purple-white vetch), all regions

Vicia villosa (hairy or winter vetch), 1

Fagaceae

Castanea pumila (chinquapin), 4, 6

Geraniaceae

Geranium richardsonii (Richardson's cranesbill or geranium), 3

Geranium spp. (cranesbills, wild geraniums), 3–5, 7

Hippocastanaceae

Aesculus californica (California buckeye or horse-chestnut), 2

Aesculus glabra (Ohio buckeye), 5

Hydophyllaceae
Eriodictyon californicum (yerba santa), 1, 2

Lamiaceae, also Labiatae
Agastache occidentalis (western giant hyssop or horse-mint), 1
*Lavandula angustifolia (lavender, English lavender), 2, 3, 5–7   MPL
*Lavandula dentata (French lavender), all regions   MPL
Marrubium vulgare (common horehound), 1, 2, 4
Mentha spp. (mints), all regions   MPL
Monarda didyma (bee-balm, Oswego-tea), 2, 7   MPL
Monarda spp. (wild bergamot, bee balms, horsemint), all regions
Monardella odoratissima (coyote mint), 1, 2
Nepeta cataria (catnip), 5–7
Prunella vulgaris (selfheal, heal-all), all regions
*Rosmarinus officinalis (rosemary), all regions   MPL
Salvia spp. (sages, salvias), all regions
*Thymus spp. (thymes), all regions

Liliaceae
Allium spp. (onions, garlics, leeks), all regions
Camassia scilloides (eastern camass, wild hyacinth), 5
Dichelostemma pulchellum (blue-dicks), 2
*Hemerocallis spp. (daylilies), all regions   MPL
Yucca filamentosa (yucca), yucca moths only, 3–7

Lobeliaceae
Lobelia cardinalis (cardinal-flower), 4, 5
*Lobelia erinus (edging lobelia), 1

Loganiaceae
*Buddleia alternifolia (fountain butterfly bush), all regions
*Buddleia davidii (orange-eye butterfly bush, summer lilac), all regions
   MPL

Malpighiaceae
Malpighia glabra (Barbados-cherry), 4

Malvaceae
*Hibiscus spp. (hibiscus), 2, 4, 6

Mimosaceae
Acacia greggii (catclaw acacia), 2, 4, 5
Albizia julibrissin (mimosa, mimosa- or silk-tree), 2, 4, 7
Pithecellobium flexicaule (Texas ebony), moths also, 4
Prosopis juliflora (mesquite), 2–4

Nyctaginaceae
*Bougainvillea spp. (bougainvilleas), 4
*Mirabilis jalapa (four-o'clock, marvel-of-Peru), moths only, 5, 6

Oleaceae
Forestiera acuminata (swamp-privet), 4
*Ligustrum spp. (privets), all regions   *MPL*
*Syringa vulgaris (common lilac), moths also, all regions

Onagraceae
Epilobium angustifolium (fireweed, great willow-herb), moths only, 1, 2
Oenothera spp. (evening primroses), moths only, 1–3

Plumbaginaceae
Limonium californicum (sea-lavender), 2
*Plumbago auriculata (Cape leadwort), 2, 5

Polemoniaceae
Gilia capitata (blue-field, blue-headed or globe gilia), 1, 2
Ipomopsis rubra (standing-cypress, Spanish-larkspur, Texas-plume),
    moths also, 3
Phlox spp. (phlox), all regions   *MPL*

Polygonaceae
Eriogonum fasciculatum (California buckwheat, flat-top buckwheat), 2
Eriogonum latifolium (broad-leaved buckwheat), 1, 2
Eriogonum umbellatum (sulfur-flower), 1–4
Eriogonum spp. (wild buckwheats), 1–5
Fagopyrum esculentum (buckwheat), 5–7
Polygonum spp. (knotweeds, smartweeds), 5–7

Pontederiaceae
Pontederia cordata (pickerelweed), 6, 7

Rhamnaceae

Ceanothus americanus (New Jersey tea), 5–7
Ceanothus cordulatus (snowbrush, mountain whitethorn), 2
Ceanothus cuneatus (buckbrush), 2
Ceanothus fendleri (Rocky mountain wild lilac), 3
Ceanothus herbaceus (prairie redroot), 5, 6
Ceanothus integerrimus (deerbrush), 2
Ceanothus sanguineus (Oregon teatree, wild lilac), 2
Ceanothus thyrsiflorus (blueblossom, wild lilac), 2

Rosaceae

Fallugia paradoxa (Apache-plume), 4
Filipendula purpurea (queen-of-the-pasture), 5–7
Fragaria virginiana (common or wild strawberry), 5–7
Physocarpus monogynus (ninebark), 3
Potentilla fruticosa (shrubby cinquefoil), 1, 3, 4, 7
Prunus angustifolia (Chickasaw plum), 6
Prunus caroliniana (Carolina laurel-cherry), 4
Prunus virginiana (chokecherry), 1–3
Rubus spp. (blackberries, dewberries, raspberries), 5–7

Rubiaceae

Cephalanthus occidentalis (buttonbush), 2, 4, 7
Houstonia caerulea (bluets), 5–7

Salicaceae

Salix discolor (pussy willow), male plants, all regions

Sapindaceae

Cardiospermum halicacabum (balloon-vine, heart-pea), 4
Sapindus saponaria (wing-leaf soapberry), 4

Saxifragaceae

Escallonia spp. (escallonia), pink and red varieties especially, 2
Philadelphus spp. (mock-oranges), 3, 5, 7

Solanaceae

Nicotiana alata (flowering tobacco), moths only, 4   *MPL*
Petunia × *hybrida* (common garden petunia), moths only, all
    regions   *MPL*

Tiliaceae
 Tilia americana (American linden, basswood), 2, 3, 5

Valerianaceae
 *Centranthus ruber (Jupiter's-beard, red valerian), 2   *MPL*

Verbenaceae
 *Lantana camara (lantana, yellow sage), orange varieties especially, 2, 4,
   6   *MPL*
 *Lantana montevidensis (trailing lantana), 2, 4, 6   *MPL*
 Phyla lanceolata (northern fog- or frogfruit), 2
 Phyla nodiflora (fog- or frogfruit, mat-grass, turkey-tangle), 2, 4, 6
 Verbena spp. (verbenas, vervains), all regions

Zygophyllaceae
 Kallstroemia grandiflora (desert poppy), 2, 4

APPENDIX B:
The Most Familiar
North American Butterflies and
Their Larval Food Plants

~

THE FOLLOWING LIST is organized by butterfly family and within each family alphabetically by genus and species. The common names appear in parentheses; in some cases, more than one common name is given. The occurrence of the butterfly is indicated by numbers representing regions according to the "Key to Geographical Regions" on page 138. Flight-time information will help the gardener know when to expect a butterfly species. Larval food plants are listed by genus and species, followed by their common names in parentheses. Note that these are widely used and current common names that may differ in your area. The abbreviation "spp." indicates that two or more species of the genus are known to attract butterflies. An "spp." usually can be taken to mean that various species in the genus potentially attract butterflies.

SWALLOWTAILS

Battus philenor   **(pipevine swallowtail)**

OCCURRENCE: resident in 2, 4, and 6; immigrant or temporary colonist in 3, 5, and 7

FLIGHT TIME: 2 broods in North, 3 in South; January–October depending on latitude, late April–early autumn in New England

LARVAL FOOD PLANTS: various species of *Aristolochia* (pipevine), including *A. durior* (Dutchman's-pipe) and *A. serpentaria* (Virginia snakeroot)

Eurytides marcellus   **(zebra swallowtail)**

OCCURRENCE: resident in 5–7 and east Texas (rare)

FLIGHT TIME: 1–3 broods, April–October; the first brood most common

LARVAL FOOD PLANTS: *Asimina* spp. (pawpaws)

Papilio cresphontes   **(giant swallowtail)**

OCCURRENCE: resident in 2 and 4–7; stray in 3

FLIGHT TIME: year-round in South in multiple broods but scarce in midwinter; May–June and August–September broods farther north produce summer and autumn individuals unpredictably throughout range

LARVAL FOOD PLANTS: *Zanthoxylum americanum* (prickly-ash) and *Z. clava-herculis* (Hercules'-club), *Ptelea trifoliata* (hop-tree), *Citrus* spp. (citrus), and *Amyris elemifera* (torchwood)

Papilio eurymedon   **(pale swallowtail)**

OCCURRENCE: resident in 1–3 and northern New Mexico

FLIGHT TIME: 1 brood, May–July

LARVAL FOOD PLANTS: *Prunus* spp. (cherries and plums), *Crataegus* spp. (hawthorns), *Holodiscus* spp. (ocean-spray, rock-spiraea), *Ceanothus* spp. (wild lilacs), *Rhamnus* spp. (buckthorns), and *Alnus oregona* (red alder)

Papilio glaucus   **(tiger swallowtail)**

OCCURRENCE: resident in 4–7 and eastern Colorado (rare)

FLIGHT TIME: 2 or 3 broods, spring–autumn; actual dates vary with latitude

LARVAL FOOD PLANTS: *Liriodendron tulipifera* (tulip-tree), *Magnolia virginiana* (sweet-bay), *Prunus serotina* (wild black cherry) and *P. vir-*

giniana (choke cherry), *Fraxinus* spp. (ashes), *Ptelea trifoliata* (hop-tree), *Carpinus caroliniana* (American hornbeam), *Lindera benzoin* (spicebush), and *Syringa vulgaris* (lilac). *Papilio canadensis* (Canadian tiger swallowtail), a single-brooded northern relative, feeds on *Betula* spp. (birches) and *Populus* spp. (aspens)

Papilio multicaudatus　(two-tailed swallowtail)

OCCURRENCE: resident in 1–4 and western part of 5

FLIGHT TIME: February–November in Texas, spring and fall broods in California, single May–August brood in Rockies and Cascades

LARVAL FOOD PLANTS: various *Prunus* spp. (wild plums), *Fraxinus* spp. (ashes), *Ptelea trifoliata* (hop-tree), and *Platanus racemosa* (western sycamore)

Papilio polyxenes　(black swallowtail)

OCCURRENCE: resident in 2–7

FLIGHT TIME: 2 or 3 broods, February–November, depending on latitude; late spring, midsummer, and early autumn flights in mid-continent

LARVAL FOOD PLANTS: various umbelliferous plants, including *Anethum graveolens* (dill), *Daucus carota* (cultivated carrot and Queen Anne's lace), *Pastinaca sativa* (wild parsnip), and *Petroselinum crispum* (parsley); various members of the Rutaceae family (Rue), including *Ruta* spp. (rues), also reported

Papilio rutulus　(western tiger swallowtail)

OCCURRENCE: resident in 1–4

FLIGHT TIME: up to 3 broods in California, 1 brood elsewhere; February in southern California, May in Washington, normally June–July in mountain areas

LARVAL FOOD PLANTS: many woody shrubs and trees, including *Prunus* spp. (wild plums and cherries), *Amelanchier* spp. (serviceberries), and *Crataegus* spp. (hawthorns), in the rose family; poplars, aspens, and willows (willow family); *Alnus* spp. (birch family); and *Platanus racemosa* (western sycamore)

Papilio troilus　(spicebush swallowtail)

OCCURRENCE: resident in 4–7; rare stray in 3

FLIGHT TIME: 2–3 broods, spring–early autumn; dates vary depending on latitude

LARVAL FOOD PLANTS: *Sassafras albidum* (sassafras) and *Lindera ben-*

zoin (spicebush) are the normal hosts; other laurel family and magnolia family hosts used on occasion

Papilio zelicaon (anise swallowtail)

OCCURRENCE: common resident in 1–3; rare in 4 and 5

FLIGHT TIME: 1 brood in most of range, May–July; 2 or 3 broods in lowland California and Northwest

LARVAL FOOD PLANTS: many umbelliferous plants, including *Foeniculum vulgare* (fennel), dill, carrot, wild parsnip, and parsley; *Citrus sinensis* (sweet orange) and other citrus eaten on occasion

WHITES AND YELLOWS

Colias eurytheme (orange sulfur)

OCCURRENCE: common in all regions

FLIGHT TIME: overlapping broods, March–December; shorter period farther north

LARVAL FOOD PLANTS: a wide variety of legumes, including *Medicago sativa* (alfalfa), *Meiilotus alba* (white sweet-clover), *Trifolium* spp. (clovers), and *Astragalus* spp. (milk-vetches)

Colias philodice (clouded sulfur, yellow sulfur)

OCCURRENCE: resident in all regions; rare in 2, 4, and 6

FLIGHT TIME: several broods, March–December, depending on weather

LARVAL FOOD PLANTS: many herbaceous legumes—a variety similar to that used by the orange sulfur

Eurema lisa (little yellow)

OCCURRENCE: resident in 4 and 6; colonist in 5 and 7

FLIGHT TIME: year-round in Deep South, May–October farther north

LARVAL FOOD PLANTS: *Cassia* spp. and some other legumes

Eurema nicippe (sleepy orange)

OCCURRENCE: resident in 2, 4, and 6; stray in 3, 5, and 7

FLIGHT TIME: 3 broods, most of the year

LARVAL FOOD PLANTS: *Cassia* spp.

Phoebis sennae (cloudless sulfur)

OCCURRENCE: resident in 2, 4, and 6; stray in 3, 5, and 7

FLIGHT TIME: multiple broods in South, 2 farther north; year-round where warm enough, midsummer to autumn where immigrant rather than resident

LARVAL FOOD PLANTS: *Cassia* spp.

Pieris rapae   (European cabbage white)

OCCURRENCE: resident in all regions; rare or absent in lowland parts of Texas and the Deep South

FLIGHT TIME: 3 or more broods, from spring thaw to first hard frost

LARVAL FOOD PLANTS: many plants in the mustard family, including *Brassica oleracea* and *B. rapa* (cabbage, turnip, kale, wild mustards); *Raphanus sativa* (radish); and a few plants in related families: caper family, including *Cleome* spp. and *Capparis* spp.; nasturtium family, including *Tropaeolum majus* (garden nasturtium) and Reseda family

Pontia protodice   (checkered white)

OCCURRENCE: resident in 2, 4, and 6; periodic colonist in other regions

FLIGHT TIME: several broods, early spring–late autumn

LARVAL FOOD PLANTS: many mustard family plants, including *Lepidium* spp. (peppergrasses), *Brassica* spp. (mustards), *Descurainia* spp. (tansy-mustards), and *Sisymbrium* spp. (tumble-mustards)

GOSSAMER WINGS

Atlides halesus   (great purple hairstreak)

OCCURRENCE: resident in 2–4, 5 (rare), and 6

FLIGHT TIME: usually 2 broods, February–October, with late summer brood more common; a third brood may occur in Deep South

LARVAL FOOD PLANTS: mistletoes (genus *Phoradendron* only)

Celastrina argiolus   (spring azure)

OCCURRENCE: resident in all regions; absent from central and south Texas

FLIGHT TIME: multiple broods on East Coast, March–August; fewer northward, 1 or 2 broods in West

LARVAL FOOD PLANTS: flowering parts of many woody trees and shrubs, including *Cornus* spp. (dogwoods), *Viburnum* spp. (viburnums), *Ceanothus americana* (New Jersey tea), and *Ligustrum* spp. (privets)

Everes comyntas   (eastern tailed blue)

OCCURRENCE: resident in 2–7; rare and local in West

FLIGHT TIME: 3 broods in North, probably more in South, often over-lapping; first flight begins in early spring

LARVAL FOOD PLANTS: many legumes, including *Astragalus* spp. (milk-vetches), *Desmodium* spp. (tick-trefoils), *Lotus* spp. (lotus), *Lathyrus* spp. and *Vicia* spp. (peas and vetches), *Trifolium* spp. (clovers), *Melilotus* spp. (sweet-clovers), and *Lupinus* spp. (lupines)

Hemiargus isolus   (Reakirt's blue)

OCCURRENCE: resident in 2, 4, and 6 (rare); immigrant and colonist in 3, 5, and 7 (rare)

FLIGHT TIME: many overlapping broods in South, June–October in North

LARVAL FOOD PLANTS: many legumes, including *Prosopis juliflora* (mesquite), *Trifolium* spp. (clovers), *Medicago sativa* (alfalfa), *Melilotus* spp. (sweet-clovers), *Indigofera* spp. (indigos), and *Dalea* spp. (indigo-bushes)

Leptotes marina   (marine blue)

OCCURRENCE: resident in 2 and 4; rare stray in 3, 5, and 6

FLIGHT TIME: multiple, continuous broods in tropics and frost-free temperate regions; peaks February–November in Southwest; summer immigrant to North

LARVAL FOOD PLANTS: many legumes, including *Prosopis juliflora* (mesquite), *Dalea* spp. (indigo-bushes), and *Medicago sativa* (alfalfa); also *Plumbago* spp. (leadworts)

Lycaeides melissa   (Melissa blue)

OCCURRENCE: resident in 1–5 and 7

FLIGHT TIME: 2 broods in East, May–mid-June and July–August; 3 broods in West, April–September

LARVAL FOOD PLANTS: Karner blue (subspecies *samuelis*) in East eats only *Lupinus perennis* (sundial lupine); in West, many legumes, including *Astragalus* spp. (milk-vetches), *Lupinus* spp. (lupines), and *Medicago sativa* (alfalfa)

Lycaena helloides   (purplish copper)

OCCURRENCE: common resident in 1–3 and 5; rare resident in parts of 4 and 7

FLIGHT TIME: multiple broods; most of year in southern California, May–early October farther north

LARVAL FOOD PLANTS: *Rumex* spp. (docks), *Polygonum* spp. (knotweeds), and *Potentilla* spp. (cinquefoils)

Lycaena phlaeas   (small copper)

OCCURRENCE: local native montane populations in 1–3; imported resident in 5–7

FLIGHT TIME: 2–4 broods in eastern half of continent; western montane and tundra populations have 1 brood in July and August

LARVAL FOOD PLANTS: in East, *Rumex* spp. (docks), especially *Rumex acetosella* (sheep sorrel); in West and Arctic, *Oxyria digyna* (mountain sorrel)

Satyrium calanus   (banded hairstreak)

OCCURRENCE: resident in 3–7

FLIGHT TIME: 1 brood, late May–early July

LARVAL FOOD PLANTS: primarily *Quercus* spp. (oaks), occasionally *Carya* spp. (hickories) and *Juglans* spp. (walnuts)

Satyrium liparops   (striped hairstreak)

OCCURRENCE: resident in 3, 5–7, and locally in east Texas

FLIGHT TIME: 1 brood, June–early August

LARVAL FOOD PLANTS: a wide variety of woody shrubs and trees, including *Prunus* spp. (wild plums), *Quercus* spp. (oaks), *Vaccinium* spp. (blueberries), and *Fraxinus* spp. (ashes)

Satyrium titus   (coral hairstreak)

OCCURRENCE: resident in all regions

FLIGHT TIME: 1 brood, late May–August, mostly in July

LARVAL FOOD PLANTS: various *Prunus* spp. (wild plums)

Strymon melinus   (gray hairstreak)

OCCURRENCE: resident in all regions; possible colonist in North

FLIGHT TIME: variable, number of broods increasing southward; 2 in North, 3 or more in South, April–October

LARVAL FOOD PLANTS: an incredibly wide variety of seed plants, especially from mallow family and legume family

BRUSHFOOTS

Agraulis vanillae   (gulf fritillary)
OCCURRENCE: resident in 2, 4, and 6; rare stray northward
FLIGHT TIME: several broods; early spring–winter in far South, summer in North where immigrant
LARVAL FOOD PLANTS: *Passiflora* spp. (passion-flowers or -vines), including *P. foetida* (running-pop), *P. incarnata* (maypops), and some ornamental species

Boloria bellona   (meadow fritillary)
OCCURRENCE: resident in 1, 3, 5 (rare), 6 (rare), and 7
FLIGHT TIME: up to 3 broods, May–September; 1 brood in Rockies and colder parts of Canada, June–July
LARVAL FOOD PLANTS: *Viola* spp. (violets), including *V. sororia* (woolly blue violet) and *V. pallens* (northern white violet)

Cercyonis pegala   (common wood nymph)
OCCURRENCE: resident in all regions
FLIGHT TIME: 1 brood, generally June–August or September, varying with locality
LARVAL FOOD PLANTS: various grasses, including *Tridens flavus* (redtop)

Chlosyne gorgone   (Gorgone crescent)
OCCURRENCE: resident in 4–6 and 7 (rare)
FLIGHT TIME: 2 broods in most of range, May–September
LARVAL FOOD PLANTS: various composites, especially *Helianthus* spp. (sunflowers)

Coenonympha tullia   (ringlet)
OCCURRENCE: resident in 1–3, 4 (rare), 5, and 7 (spreading)
FLIGHT TIME: 1 brood in most of range, May–July; several broods in California, February–October
LARVAL FOOD PLANTS: grasses, the specific kinds mainly unreported

Danaus gilippus   (queen)
OCCURRENCE: resident in warmer parts of 2, 4, and 6; vagrant in 3, 5, and 7 (rare)
FLIGHT TIME: successive broods, April–November; briefer in North, perhaps all year in south Texas

LARVAL FOOD PLANTS: milkweed family, especially *Asclepias* spp. (milkweeds) in the U.S.

Danaus plexippus (monarch)
OCCURRENCE: annual colonist in all regions; resident in 2 and 6; coastal California and central Mexican highlands, October–March
FLIGHT TIME: successive broods; migrating northward from March to June, resident in North from July to August, migrates southward from August to October, resident rest of year in overwintering locales; year-round resident in southern California and Hawaii
LARVAL FOOD PLANTS: *Asclepias* spp. (milkweeds)

Euptoieta claudia (variegated fritillary)
OCCURRENCE: resident in 2, 4, and 6; colonist in 3, 5, and 7
FLIGHT TIME: continuous broods, spring–autumn
LARVAL FOOD PLANTS: a wide variety of plants, especially *Viola* spp. (violets and pansies)

Heliconius charitonius (zebra)
OCCURRENCE: resident in 4 and 6; stray in 2 and 5
FLIGHT TIME: multiple broods; year-round in Florida, except when colder weather occurs
LARVAL FOOD PLANTS: *Passiflora* spp. (passion-flowers or -vines)

Junonia coenia (buckeye)
OCCURRENCE: resident in 2, 4, and 6; stray or colonist in all other regions
FLIGHT TIME: 2–4 broods; year-round in Deep South, elsewhere March–October
LARVAL FOOD PLANTS: *Plantago* spp. (plantains); *Phyla nodiflora* (fogfruit); several snapdragon family plants, including common *Antirrhinum majus* (snapdragon) and *Agalinus* spp. (gerardias, false foxgloves); and *Ruellia* spp. (wild petunias)

Libytheana carinenta (snout butterfly)
OCCURRENCE: resident in 2, 4, and 6; stray or colonist in 3, 5, and 7
FLIGHT TIME: 3 or more broods; February or March in South, later farther north, year-round in extreme southern part of range
LARVAL FOOD PLANTS: *Celtis* spp. (hackberry trees)

Limenitis archippus   (viceroy)

OCCURRENCE: resident in all regions

FLIGHT TIME: 2 or more broods depending on latitude; April–September in middle latitudes, later in South; sometimes a distinct gap between broods, with no adults for some weeks in mid- to late summer

LARVAL FOOD PLANTS: *Salix* spp. (willows) and *Populus* spp. (cottonwoods)

Limenitis arthemis arthemis   (banded admiral)

OCCURRENCE: resident in 3 (rare), 5, and 7

FLIGHT TIME: 1 or 2 broods, June–August

LARVAL FOOD PLANTS: primarily *Betula* spp. (birches), especially *B. lenta* (black birch) and *B. alleghaniensis* (yellow birch), and *Populus* spp. (aspens), but also a few other woody shrubs and trees

Limenitis arthemis astyanax   (red-spotted purple)

OCCURRENCE: resident in 2 and 4–7

FLIGHT TIME: 2 broods in North, up to 3 broods in Deep South, mid-spring through late summer

LARVAL FOOD PLANTS: usually *Prunus serotina* (wild black cherry) and *P. virginiana* (choke cherry), but also *Populus* spp. (poplars) and *Quercus* spp. (oaks)

Limenitis lorquini   (Lorquin's admiral)

OCCURRENCE: resident in 1–3

FLIGHT TIME: 2 broods in California, April–September; 1 brood in Northwest, June–September

LARVAL FOOD PLANTS: *Salix* spp. (willows), *Populus* spp. (poplars and aspens), *Prunus* spp. (wild plums), and a few woody shrubs

Limenitis weidemeyeri   (Weidemeyer's admiral)

OCCURRENCE: resident in 1 (rare), 2–4, and 5 (rare)

FLIGHT TIME: 1 or 2 broods, late May–September

LARVAL FOOD PLANTS: *Salix* spp. (willows), *Populus* spp. (aspens and poplars), *Prunus virginiana* (choke cherry), *Amelanchier* spp. (serviceberries), and *Holodiscus* spp. (ocean-spray, rock-spiraea)

Nymphalis antiopa   (mourning cloak)

OCCURRENCE: resident in all regions

FLIGHT TIME: usually only a single brood, occasionally a second; long-lived adults found year-round, most commonly in spring and early summer

LARVAL FOOD PLANTS: *Salix* spp. (willows), *Populus* spp. (aspens and cottonwoods), and *Ulmus* spp. (elms)

Nymphalis milberti   (Milbert's tortoise shell)

OCCURRENCE: resident in 1–5, 6 (rare), and 7

FLIGHT TIME: 2 or 3 broods where length of growing season permits, spring—autumn

LARVAL FOOD PLANTS: *Urtica* spp. (nettles)

Phyciodes campestris   (field crescent)

OCCURRENCE: resident in 1–3; rare in 4 and 5

FLIGHT TIME: 1–3 broods, mostly May–September; June–August in higher mountains and Canada

LARVAL FOOD PLANTS: primarily *Aster* spp. (asters)

Phyciodes mylitta   (mylitta crescent)

OCCURRENCE: resident in 1–4

FLIGHT TIME: several overlapping broods, March–October

LARVAL FOOD PLANTS: *Cirsium* spp. (thistles) and related plants

Phyciodes phaon   (phaon crescent)

OCCURRENCE: resident in 2, 4, and 6; stray or temporary colonist in 3 and 5

FLIGHT TIME: 2 or more broods, April–September, year-round in tropics

LARVAL FOOD PLANTS: *Phyla lanceolata* (fogfruit) and *P. nodiflora* (mat-grass)

Phyciodes tharos   (pearl crescent)

OCCURRENCE: resident in 2–7

FLIGHT TIME: several broods, March–November; *Phyciodes pascoenis*, the related northern pearl crescent of the northern United States and Canada, has 1 brood, June–August

LARVAL FOOD PLANTS: *Aster* spp. (asters)

Polygonia comma   (comma, hop merchant)

OCCURRENCE: resident in 3 (rare), 4 (rare), and 5–7

FLIGHT TIME: 2 broods in North, 3 farther south, March or April until late fall; adults overwinter

LARVAL FOOD PLANTS: *Urtica* spp. (nettles), *Laportea canadensis* (wood-nettle), *Boehmeria* spp. (false-nettles), *Ulmus americana* (American elm), and *Humulus* spp. (hops)

Polygonia interrogationis   (question mark)
OCCURRENCE: resident in 3–7; rare in southeastern Arizona
FLIGHT TIME: 2 or 3 broods, spring to autumn; overwinters as adult and migrates
LARVAL FOOD PLANTS: *Urtica* spp. (nettles), *Boehmeria* spp. (false-nettles), *Ulmus* spp. (elms), *Humulus* spp. (hops), and *Celtis* spp. (hackberries)

Polygonia progne   (gray comma)
OCCURRENCE: resident in 3 and 5–7
FLIGHT TIME: 2 broods, April–October; adults overwinter
LARVAL FOOD PLANTS: *Ribes* spp. (gooseberries), *Rhododendron* spp. (rhododendrons), occasionally *Betula papyrifera* (paper birch)

Speyeria aphrodite   (Aphrodite fritillary)
OCCURRENCE: resident in 2 (rare), 3, 4 (rare), and 5–7
FLIGHT TIME: 1 brood, June–September
LARVAL FOOD PLANTS: *Viola* spp. (violets)

Speyeria cybele   (great spangled fritillary)
OCCURRENCE: resident in 1–3, 4 (rare), and 5–7
FLIGHT TIME: 1 brood, June–September
LARVAL FOOD PLANTS: *Viola* spp. (violets)

Vanessa annabella   (West Coast lady)
OCCURRENCE: resident in 1–4; stray in 5
FLIGHT TIME: year-round in coastal California, elsewhere spottily from early spring–late autumn, autumn in eastern part of range
LARVAL FOOD PLANTS: mallow family plants, including *Alcea rosea* (hollyhock), occasionally *Urtica* spp. (nettles)

Vanessa atalanta   (red admiral)
OCCURRENCE: resident or colonist in all regions
FLIGHT TIME: 2 broods in most of range; generally April or May–October, year-round in Deep South; migrates
LARVAL FOOD PLANTS: nettle family plants, including *Urtica* spp. (nettles); occasionally *Humulus* spp. (hops)

Vanessa cardui   (painted lady)

OCCURRENCE: regular or periodic migrant and colonist in all regions

FLIGHT TIME: 2 or more broods; all year in southern deserts, April–June until hard frosts in North

LARVAL FOOD PLANTS: a wide variety of plants in many families, primarily composites, legumes, borages, and nettles

Vanessa virginiensis   (American painted lady)

OCCURRENCE: resident or colonist in all regions

FLIGHT TIME: 2 or 3 broods, summer–autumn

LARVAL FOOD PLANTS: primarily *Gnaphalium* spp., *Antennaria* spp., and *Anaphalis margaritacea* (everlastings); occasionally other herbaceous plants

SKIPPERS

Achalarus lyciades   (hoary edge)

OCCURRENCE: resident in 4, 5 (rare), 6, and 7

FLIGHT TIME: 1 brood in North, May–August; 2 broods in Deep South, April–September

LARVAL FOOD PLANTS: primarily *Desmodium* spp. (tick-trefoils)

Atalopedes campestris   (sachem)

OCCURRENCE: resident in 2, 4, and 6; stray or colonist in 3, 5, and 7

FLIGHT TIME: 3 broods in South, most of year; May–October in North where immigrant

LARVAL FOOD PLANTS: *Cynodon dactylon* (Bermuda grass) and other similar grasses

Epargyreus clarus   (silver-spotted skipper)

OCCURRENCE: resident in all regions

FLIGHT TIME: 1 brood in North and West, 2 broods in South, May–September

LARVAL FOOD PLANTS: several legumes, including *Robinia* spp. (locust trees) and *Wisteria* spp. (wisterias)

Euphyes vestris   (dun skipper)

OCCURRENCE: resident in 2–7

FLIGHT TIME: 1 brood, late May–July

LARVAL FOOD PLANTS: *Carex* spp. (sedges)

Hylephila phyleus   (fiery skipper)
OCCURRENCE: resident in 2, 4, and 6; rare stray or colonist in all other regions
FLIGHT TIME: 2 or more broods, April–September in coastal California and South, shorter period northward
LARVAL FOOD PLANTS: *Cynodon dactylon* (Bermuda grass), *Poa* spp. (bluegrasses), and other grasses

Ochlodes sylvanoides   (woodland skipper)
OCCURRENCE: resident in 1–3; rare in 4
FLIGHT TIME: 1 brood, usually July–October
LARVAL FOOD PLANTS: *Cynodon dactylon* (Bermuda grass) and a few other grasses

Pholisora catullus   (common sooty wing)
OCCURRENCE: resident or colonist in all regions
FLIGHT TIME: 2 broods, March–November
LARVAL FOOD PLANTS: *Chenopodium album* (lamb's-quarters) and *Amaranthus* spp. (amaranths) are especially favored

Poanes hobomok   (northern golden skipper)
OCCURRENCE: resident in 3 (rare) and 5–7
FLIGHT TIME: 1 extended brood, June–July
LARVAL FOOD PLANTS: grasses, including *Panicum* spp. (panic grasses) and *Poa* spp. (bluegrasses)

Poanes taxiles   (golden skipper)
OCCURRENCE: resident in 2–4 and 5 (rare)
FLIGHT TIME: 1 brood, June–July
LARVAL FOOD PLANTS: various grasses

Poanes zabulon   (southern golden skipper)
OCCURRENCE: resident in 5–7
FLIGHT TIME: 2 broods, May–September; may appear as early as March in Deep South
LARVAL FOOD PLANTS: grasses, including *Tridens flavus* (redtop) and *Eragrostis* spp. (lovegrasses)

Polites peckius   (yellow patch skipper, Peck's skipper)
OCCURRENCE: resident in 1, 3, and 5–7
FLIGHT TIME: 2 broods, May–September

LARVAL FOOD PLANTS: grasses, likely including *Poa pratensis* (Kentucky bluegrass)

Polites sabuleti   (sandhill skipper)
OCCURRENCE: resident in 1–4
FLIGHT TIME: 2 broods in most areas, 1 brood in mountains, May–September
LARVAL FOOD PLANTS: grasses, including *Distichlis* spp. (saltgrasses), *Cynodon dactylon* (Bermuda grass), and *Poa* spp. (bluegrasses)

Polites themistocles   (tawny-edged skipper)
OCCURRENCE: resident in all regions
FLIGHT TIME: 2 broods, May–August
LARVAL FOOD PLANTS: *Poa pratensis* (Kentucky bluegrass), *Panicum* spp. (panic grasses), and others

Pyrgus communis   (checkered skipper)
OCCURRENCE: resident or colonist in all regions
FLIGHT TIME: successive broods; year-round in Deep South, April–October northward
LARVAL FOOD PLANTS: many mallow family plants

Thymelicus lineola   (European skipper)
OCCURRENCE: rare resident in 1 and 3; common resident in 5–7
FLIGHT TIME: 1 brood, June–August
LARVAL FOOD PLANTS: grasses, especially *Phleum pratense* (timothy)

Urbanus proteus   (tailed skipper)
OCCURRENCE: resident in 4 and 6 (rare); stray in 2, 5, and 7
FLIGHT TIME: 2 or 3 broods, flies all year in Deep South
LARVAL FOOD PLANTS: various legumes, including *Phaseolus* spp. (beans), *Desmodium* spp. (tick-trefoils), and others

Wallengrenia egeremet   (northern broken dash)
OCCURRENCE: resident in 4–7
FLIGHT TIME: 1 brood in North, June–August; 2 broods in Deep South, April–September
LARVAL FOOD PLANTS: *Panicum* spp. (panic grasses)

Wallengrenia otho   (broken dash)
OCCURRENCE: resident in 4, 5, 6, and southeastern part of 7 (rare)
FLIGHT TIME: 2 or 3 broods, March–September
LARVAL FOOD PLANTS: various grasses

RESURCES

~

Parts of this section were adapted, with permission, from *The Butterfly Garden*, by Mathew Tekulsky (Boston: Harvard Common Press, 1985).

ENTOMOLOGICAL EQUIPMENT AND BOOKS

The following companies offer butterflies and moths, educational kits, and books for sale. For further sources, you can consult newsletters and other publications of conservation and gardening societies. (See the next section, "Conservation and Gardening Organizations.")

American Biological Supply Company
1330 Dillon Heights Avenue
Baltimore, MD 21228
(301) 747-1797
   Free catalog upon request.

BioQuip Products
17803 LaSalle Avenue
Gardena, CA 90248
(213) 324-0620
   Price list upon request.

Carolina Biological Supply Company
2700 York Road
Burlington, NC 27215
(800) 632-1231 (in NC)
(800) 334-5551 (rest of U.S.)
   Catalog: $15.75 (free to schools, companies, and libraries).

Connecticut Valley Biological Supply Company
82 Valley Road
P.O. Box 326

Southampton, MA 01073
(800) 649-4030 (in MA)
(800) 628-7748 (rest of U.S.)
   Free catalog upon request.

Entomological Society of America
9301 Annapolis Road
Lanham, MD 20706
(301) 731-4535
   Free book catalog upon request.

Insect Lore Products
P.O. Box 1535
Shafter, CA 93263
(800) LIVE-BUG
   Free catalog upon request.

John Staples
Breeder of Lepidoptera
389 Rock Beach Road
Rochester, NY 14617
(716) 544-8198
   Price list upon request.

Nasco
901 Janesville Avenue
Fort Atkinson, WI 53538
   or
Nasco West
1524 Princeton Avenue
Modesto, CA 95352
(800) 558-9595
   Free science catalog upon request.

Ward's Natural Sciences Establishment
5100 West Henrietta Road
P.O. Box 92912
Rochester, NY 14692
   or
Ward's Natural Sciences Establishment
11850 East Florence Avenue
Santa Fe Springs, CA 90670
(800) 962-2660
   Catalog: $15.00 (free to schools, companies, and libraries).

CONSERVATION AND GARDENING ORGANIZATIONS

Butterflies, Moths, and Insects

American Entomological Society
1900 Race Street
Philadelphia, PA 19013
(215) 561-3978
   Annual dues: $5.00. Publishes Transactions of the American Entomological Society, Memoirs of the American Entomological Society, *and* Entomological News.

Butterfly Lovers International
Dr. Stevanne Auerbach, Director
210 Columbus Avenue
San Francisco, CA 94133
(415) 864-1169

Entomological Society of America
9301 Annapolis Road
Lanham, MD 20706
(301) 731-4535
   Annual dues: students, $20.00; regular membership, $60.00. Publishes The American Entomologist, Annals of the Entomological Society of America, Journal of Economic Entomology, Journal of Medical Entomology, Miscellaneous Publications of the Entomological Society of America, *and* Environmental Entomology.

The Lepidoptera Research Foundation
c/o Santa Barbara Museum of Natural History
2559 Puesta Del Sol Road
Santa Barbara, CA 93105
(805) 682-4711
   Publishes The Journal of Research on the Lepidoptera.

The Lepidopterists' Society
Dr. William D. Winter, Secretary
257 Common Street
Dedham, MA 02026-4020
(617) 326-6053
   Annual dues: $25.00; open to anyone interested in Lepidoptera. Publishes News of the Lepidopterists' Society, Journal of the Lepidopterists' Soci-

ety, *and* Memoirs of the Lepidopterists' Society. *(The "Market Place" col-*
umn in the News of the L. S. *contains classified advertisements for butterfly*
eggs and pupae as well as moth eggs and cocoons.)

National Wildlife Federation
Urban Wildlife Programs
1400 16th St. N.W.
Washington, DC 20036-2266
(202) 797-6800

Publications: The Gardening with Wildlife Kit *($19.95) includes simple*
instructions and planning tools for creating a backyard sanctuary for butterflies,
birds, and other animals; The Backyard Naturalist *($7.95), by Craig Tufts,*
director of NWF's Urban Wildlife Programs, includes sections on butterflies.
The Federation's Backyard Wildlife Habitat Program provides certification and
consultation for people who want to plan their landscaping with the needs of wild-
life in mind.

Ohio Lepidopterists
Eric H. Metzler
1241 Kildale Square North
Columbus, OH 43229
(614) 265-6774

Annual dues: $7.50. Publishes The Ohio Lepidopterist.

Society of Kentucky Lepidopterists
Dr. Charles V. Covell, Jr., Secretary
Department of Biology
University of Louisville
Louisville, KY 40292
(502) 588-5942

Annual dues: $5.00. Publishes Kentucky Lepidopterist.

Sonoran Arthropod Studies, Inc.
Steve Prchal, Founder and Director
P.O. Box 5624
Tucson, AZ 85703
(602) 884-7274

Annual dues: individual, $20.00. Publishes Backyard Bug Watching *and*
Instar, *a pamphlet of events.*

Southern Lepidopterists' Society
Thomas Neal, Secretary-Treasurer
3820 Northwest Sixteenth Place

Gainesville, FL 32605
(904) 375-1916
   Annual dues: $5.00. Publishes Southern Lepidopterists' News.

Utah Lepidopterists' Society
Colonel Clyde Gillette
3419 El Serrito Drive
Salt Lake City, UT 84109
(801) 484-5804
   Annual dues: $10.00. Publishes Utahensis.

The Xerces Society
10 Southwest Ash Street
Portland, OR 97204
(503) 222-2788
   Annual dues: regular membership, $25.00. Publishes Wings: Essays on Invertebrate Conservation *three times a year, the results of the North American Fourth of July Butterfly Count, and* Atala, *a journal of invertebrate ecology, published occasionally.*

Young Entomologists' Society
International Headquarters
1915 Peggy Place
Lansing, MI 48910
(517) 887-0499
   Annual dues: $10.00. Publishes Young Entomologists' Society Quarterly. *(The "Trading Post" column in* Young Entomologists' Society Quarterly *includes live stock offered for sale and exchange.)*

Plants

Gardening by Mail 2
Barbara J. Barton
Tusker Press, 1987
   This book is a directory of mail-order resources for gardeners in the United States and Canada. Includes lists of seed companies, nurseries, suppliers of all garden necessities, and useful books about plants and gardening. Price: $16.00, paperback.

National Wildflower Research Center (NWRC)
2600 FM 973 North
Austin, TX 78725
(512) 929-3600

The library of the NWRC information clearinghouse serves as a national resource center for information on when and how to plant wildflowers; where to find seed and nursery-grown plants; and establishment and management techniques. Much of this information is also available in their publications, which include Wildflowers Across America *(New York: Abbeville Press, 1988). (See* "Wildflowers in the Planned Landscape" *by David K. Northington, p. 111.)*

The New England Wild Flower Society
Garden in the Woods
Hemenway Road
Framingham, MA 01701
(508) 877-7630

Publishes Botanical Clubs and Native Plant Societies of the United States, *which contains listings for most states. Price: $6.95, including postage and handling.*

The Soil Conservation Society of America
7515 Northeast Ankeny Road
Ankeny, IA 50021
(515) 289-2331

Publishes Sources of Native Seeds and Plants, *which contains the names and addresses of growers and suppliers of native vegetation in forty states and Canada. Price: $3.50, including postage and handling.*

LIST OF BUTTERFLY SHOWPLACES AND INSECT ZOOS

Below is a partial list of butterfly showplaces and insect zoos. For more information, write to the Young Entomologists' Society, International Headquarters, 1915 Peggy Place, Lansing, MI 48910.

Butterfly Exhibit
Marine World Africa-USA
Marine World Parkway
(Junction of I-80 and California 37)
Vallejo, CA 94589
(707) 643-6722

Call for up-to-date admission information.

Butterfly World
Tradewinds Park South
3600 West Sample Road

Coconut Creek, FL 33073
(305) 977-4400
   Admission charge; open all year except Christmas and Thanksgiving.

Day Butterfly Center
Callaway Gardens
Pine Mountain, GA 31822
(404) 663-5102
   Admission charge.

Insect Zoo
Smithsonian Institution
National Museum of Natural History
Tenth and Constitution Avenues, N.W.
Washington, DC 20560
(202) 357-1386

Invertebrate Exhibit
National Zoological Park
Smithsonian Institution
Washington, DC 20008
(202) 673-4717

SASI Insect Zoo
2437 North Stone Avenue
Tucson, AZ 85703
   Sponsored by Sonoran Arthropod Studies, Inc. Small admission charge; open all year, Tuesday–Saturday.

World of Insects Exhibit
Cincinnati Zoo
3400 Vine Street
Cincinnati, OH 45220
(513) 281-4701

BIBLIOGRAPHY

~

Parts of this bibliography were adapted, with permission, from *The Butterfly Garden*, by Mathew Tekulsky (Boston: Harvard Common Press, 1985).

BUTTERFLIES

Ackerman, Diane. "Mass Meeting on the Coast: The Glorious Off-season of the Monarch Butterfly." *Life* (May 1987): 21+.

Baldwin, Robert F. "The Butterfly Man: Down-Easter Paul Grey's Passion for Butterflies Has Led to Some Significant Findings." *Country Journal* (March 1988): 35–40.

Barbour, Spider. "Overnight Sensation." *Natural History* (May 1989): 24–29.

Bender, Steve. "Butterflies: Nature's Music on the Wing." *Southern Living* (June 1987): 56+.

Boling, Rick. "Woodsman, Spare That Butterfly." *Sierra* (July–August 1986): 100–101.

Brewer, Jo. *Wings in the Meadow*. Boston: Houghton Mifflin, 1967.

Brewer, Jo, and Dave Winter. *Butterflies and Moths: A Companion to Your Field Guide*. New York: Prentice Hall Press, 1986.

Brower, Lincoln P. "Ecological Chemistry." *Scientific American* 220, no. 2 (1969): 22–29.

———. "Monarch Migration." *Natural History* (June–July 1977).

Bruno, Mary. "On the Wings of Butterflies: Colorful Scales Aid Butterflies and Moths in Everything from Flying to Eluding Enemies." *International Wildlife* (July–August 1986): 14–19.

"Butterflies Mingle with Plants and People." *BioScience* (December 1988): 809.

"Butterfly Hide-and-Seek." *Science News* (September 20, 1986): 184.

Carter, Patrick A., and Kathleen Donohue. "Females' Choice of 'Good Geno-types' as Mates Is Promoted by an Insect Mating System." *Science* (September 12, 1986): 1187–90.

"Caterpillars Earn Their Wings." *World* (April 1989): 1252–3.

Chew, F. S. "Coexistence and Local Extinction in Two *Pieris* Butterflies." *American Naturalist* 118 (1981): 655–72.

Christensen, James R. *A Field Guide to the Butterflies of the Pacific Northwest*. Moscow: The University Press of Idaho, 1981.

Clark, Tim. "The Berth of the Blues." *Yankee* (May 1986): 20 + .

Covell, Charles V., Jr. *A Field Guide to the Moths of Eastern North America*. Boston: Houghton Mifflin, 1981.

Darlington, Elizabeth. "Those Racing, Chasing Butterflies." *Conservationist* (July–August 1988): 32–35.

Davies, John. "Butterflies Aren't Free at LAX." *Journal of Commerce and Commercial* (June 14, 1985): 1A + .

Dirig, Robert. "Nabokov's Blue Snowflakes." *Natural History* (May 1988): 68–69.

Donahue, Julian P. "Strategies for Survival: The Cause of a Caterpillar." *Terra* 17, no. 4 (1979): 3–9.

Dornfeld, Ernst J. *The Butterflies of Oregon*. Beaverton, Oreg.: Timber Press, 1980.

Douglas, Matthew M. *The Lives of Butterflies*. Ann Arbor: University of Michigan Press, 1986.

Ebner, James A. *The Butterflies of Wisconsin*. Milwaukee: Milwaukee Public Museum, 1970.

Ehrlich, Paul R., and Anne H. Ehrlich. *How to Know the Butterflies*. Dubuque, Iowa: William C. Brown, 1961.

Ely, Charles A. "An Annotated List of the Butterflies of Kansas." Fort Hays Studies, Third Series; *Science*, no. 7 (1986).

Emmel, Thomas C. *Butterflies: Their World, Their Life Cycle, Their Behavior*. New York: Alfred A. Knopf, 1975.

Emmel, Thomas C., and John F. Emmel. *The Butterflies of Southern California*. Los Angeles: Natural History Museum of Los Angeles County, 1973.

Ferguson, D. C. *Host Records for Lepidoptera Reared in Eastern North America*. Technical Bulletin no. 1521. Washington, D.C.: U.S. Department of Agriculture, Agricultural Research Service, 1975.

Ferris, Clifford D., and Martin F. Brown, eds. *Butterflies of the Rocky Mountain States*. Norman: University of Oklahoma Press, 1981.

Ford, E. B. *Butterflies*. Rev. ed. Glasgow, Scotland: Collins, 1975.

Free, J. B., Dorothy Gennard, J. H. Stevenson, and Ingrid H. Williams. "Beneficial Insects Present on a Motorway Verge." *Biological Conservation* 8 (1975): 61–72.

Garth, John S., and J. W. Tilden. *California Butterflies*. Berkeley and Los Angeles: University of California Press, 1986.

Grossman, Joel. "From Caterpillar to Butterfly." *Flower and Garden* (April—May 1986): 61–62.

Harris, Lucien, Jr. *Butterflies of Georgia*. Norman: University of Oklahoma Press, 1972.

Heitzman, J. Richard, and Joan E. Heitzman. *Butterflies and Moths of Missouri*. Jefferson County: Missouri Department of Conservation, 1987.

Hogue, Charles L. "Butterfly Wings: Living Pointillism." *Los Angeles County Museum of Natural History Quarterly* 6, no. 4 (1968): 4–11.

Hollander, Ron. "U.S. Wildlife in Peril." *Town and Country* (March 1985): 124+.

Hooper, Ronald. *Butterflies of Saskatchewan*. Regina, Canada: Saskatchewan Museum of Natural History, 1973.

Howe, Robert W. "Wings Over the Prairie." *Iowa Conservationist* (September 1984).

Howe, William H., ed. *The Butterflies of North America*. Garden City, N.Y.: Doubleday, 1975.

Irwin, Roderick, and John C. Downey. "Checklist of Butterflies of Illinois." *Illinois Natural History Survey, Biological Notes*, no. 81 (1973).

Jackson, Lawrence. "On Oxen Pond." *Nature Canada* (Summer 1987): 35–37.

Kingsolver, Joel G. "Butterfly Engineering." *Scientific American* (August 1985): 106–13.

Klassen, P., A. R. Westwood, W. B. Preston, and W. B. McKillop. *The Butterflies of Manitoba*. Winnipeg, Canada: Manitoba Museum of Man and Nature, 1989.

Klots, Alexander B. *A Field Guide to the Butterflies of North America, East of the Great Plains*. Boston: Houghton Mifflin, 1951.

Klots, Alexander B., and Elsie B. Klots. *1001 Answers to Questions About Insects*. New York: Grosset & Dunlap, 1961.

Layberry, Ross A., J. Donald LaFontaine, and P. Hall. "Butterflies of the Ottawa District." *Trail and Landscape* 16, no. 1 (1980): 3–59.

Miller, Lee D., and Martin F. Brown. *A Catalogue/Checklist of the Butterflies of America North of Mexico. Memoirs of the Lepidopterists' Society*, no. 2 (1981).

Milne, Louis, and Margery Milne. *The Audubon Society Field Guide to North American Insects and Spiders*. New York: Alfred A. Knopf, 1980.

Mitchell, Robert T., and Herbert S. Zim. *Butterflies and Moths*. Rev. ed. New York: Golden Press, 1985.

Murphy, Jamie. "Protecting a Royal Refuge: Mexico Tries to Save the Monarch Butterfly's Winter Hideout." *Time* (November 14, 1986): 89.

Nabokov, Vladimir. "Butterflies." In *Speak, Memory: An Autobiography Revisited*. New York: G. P. Putnam's Sons, 1966.

Nijhout, Frederik H. "Pattern and Pattern Diversity on Lepidopteran Wings." *BioScience* (September 1986): 527–33.

Norman, Colin. "Mexico Acts to Protect Overwintering Monarchs." *Science* (September 19, 1986): 1252–3.

Opler, Paul A., and George O. Krizek. *Butterflies East of the Great Plains*. Baltimore: Johns Hopkins University Press, 1984.

Opler, Paul A., and Susan Strawn. *Butterflies of the American West: A Coloring Album*. Boulder, Colo.: Roberts Rinehart, 1988.

———. *Butterflies of Eastern North America: A Coloring Album and Activity Book*. Boulder, Colo.: Roberts Rinehart, 1989.

Ordish, George. *The Year of the Butterfly*. New York: Charles Scribner's Sons, 1975.

Orsak, Larry J. "Buckwheat and the Bright Blue Copper." *Garden* (January–February 1980).

———. *The Butterflies of Orange County, California*. Irvine: University of California, Irvine, Press, 1977.

Panzer, Ron. "Managing Prairie Remnants for Insect Conservation." *Natural Areas Journal* 8, no. 2 (1988): 83–90.

Parenti, Umberto. *The World of Butterflies and Moths*. New York: G. P. Putnam's Sons, 1978.

Peterson, Roger Tory, Robert Michael Pyle, and Sarah Anne Hughes. *A Field Guide to Butterflies Coloring Book*. Boston: Houghton Mifflin, 1983.

Preston-Mafham, Rod, and Ken Preston-Mafham. *Butterflies of the World*. New York: Facts on File, 1988.

Pyle, Robert Michael. *The Audubon Society Field Guide to North American Butterflies*. New York: Alfred A. Knopf, 1981.

————. *The Audubon Society Handbook for Butterfly Watchers: A Guide to Observing, Locating, Identifying, Studying, and Photographing Butterflies*. New York: Charles Scribner's Sons, 1984.

————. "Butterflies: Now You See Them. . . ." *International Wildlife* (January–February 1981).

————. "Conservation of Lepidoptera in the United States." *Biological Conservation* 9 (1976): 55–75.

————. "How to Conserve Insects for Fun and Necessity." *Terra* 17, no. 4 (1979): 18–22.

————. *Watching Washington Butterflies*. Seattle: Seattle Audubon Society, 1974.

Pyle, Robert Michael, M. Bentzien, and Paul Opler. "Insect Conservation." *Annual Review of Entomology* 26 (1981): 233–58.

Royer, Ronald A. "The Butterflies of North Dakota." *Science Monograph* no. 1. Minot, N. Dak.: Minot State University, 1988.

Sbordoni, Valerio, and Saverio Forestiero. *Butterflies of the World*. Translated from Italian by Neil Stratton, Hugh Young, and Bruce Penman. New York: Times Books, 1985.

Scott, James A. *The Butterflies of North America: A Natural History and Field Guide*. Stanford, Calif.: Stanford University Press, 1986.

Shapiro, Arthur M. "Butterflies of New York State." *Search* (Cornell University) 4, no. 3 (1974).

Shissler, Byron P., and Mark E. Holman. "Wildlife Planning in Parks: A Continuing Challenge." *Parks and Recreation* (November 1985): 33–38.

Shoumatoff, Alex. "A Reporter at Large: The Skipper and the Dam." *New Yorker* (December 1, 1986): 71–84.

Shull, Ernest H. *Butterflies of Indiana*. Bloomington, Ind.: Indiana University Press, 1988.

Singer, Michael C., and Lawrence E. Gilbert. "Ecology of Butterflies in the Urbs and Suburbs." In *Perspectives in Urban Entomology*. New York: Academic Press, 1978.

Smart, Paul. *The Illustrated Encyclopedia of the Butterfly World*. New York: Chartwell Books, 1984.

Sonntag, Linda. *Butterflies*. New York: G. P. Putnam's Sons, 1980.

Stewart, Margaret M., and Claudia Ricci. "Dearth of the Blues: Butterflies That Have Thrived Since the Ice Age Are Now Endangered by Suburban Sprawl." *Natural History* (May 1988): 64–71.

Tekulsky, Mathew. "Butterflies Are Free: Where to Go Find Them." *Los Angeles Times*, *You* (September 27, 1977).

Tietz, Harrison M. *An Index to the Described Life Histories, Early Stages and Hosts of the Macrolepidoptera of the Continental United States and Canada*. 2 vols. Sarasota, Fla.: Allyn Museum of Entomology, 1972.

Tilden, J. W. *Butterflies of the San Francisco Bay Region*. Berkeley and Los Angeles: University of California Press, 1965.

Tilden, J. W., and Arthur C. Smith. *A Field Guide to Western Butterflies*. Boston: Houghton Mifflin, 1986.

Toner, Mike. "The Hidden Strength of Gossamer Wings." *National Wildlife* (August–September 1988): 4–11.

Tyler, Hamilton A. *The Swallowtail Butterflies of North America*. Healdsburg, Calif.: Naturegraph, 1975.

Urquhart, Frederick A. *The Monarch Butterfly*. Toronto: University of Toronto Press, 1960.

————. *The Monarch Butterfly: International Traveller*. Chicago: Nelson Hall, 1987.

Vane-Wright, Richard I., and Phillip R. Ackery, eds. *The Biology of Butterflies*. Symposium of the Royal Entomological Society Series. London and Orlando, Fla.: Academic Press, 1984.

Walker, Betty. "A Peep into the World of Small Things." *Canadian Geographic* (April–May 1985): 42–48.

Watson, Allan, and Paul E. S. Whalley. *The Dictionary of Butterflies and Moths in Color*. New York: Simon & Schuster, 1983.

Williams, Ted. "Butterflies Are Full of Surprises." *National Wildlife* (August–September 1979).

Xerces Society. *The Common Names of North American Butterflies*. Washington, D.C.: Smithsonian Institution Press, in press.

Zuckerman, Jim. "Monarchs by the Millions: Crowds of Monarch Butterflies Make 2,000-Mile Migrations between Mexico and the United States Twice a Year." *Americas* (September–October 1986): 16+.

BUTTERFLY GARDENING

Aliensen, Ron. "Flying Flowers." *Blair & Ketchum's Country Journal* (August 1985): 32–36.

Birke, L. "Butterflies Make the Best Use of Sunshine." *New Science* (December 17, 1988).

Borkin, Susan Sullivan. "Plant a Butterfly Garden." *Lore* 34, no. 2 (1984): 7–11.

Brewer, Jo. "Bringing Butterflies to the Garden." *Horticulture* (May 1979).

———. "Butterfly Gardening." *Xerces Society Self-Help Sheet No. 7* (1982).

———. "How to Attract Butterflies." *Horticulture* (July 1969).

———. "An Invitation to the Butterfly Meadow." *Defenders* (August 1978).

"Butterflies for Sale." *Dun's Business Month* (May 1984).

"Butterflies Mingle with Plants and People." *BioScience* (December 1988).

Byers, P. "*Buddleia*, the Butterfly Bush." *Flower & Garden* (June–July 1986).

Cervoni, Cleti. "Butterfly Gardens." *Essex Life* (Spring 1985).

Collman, Sharon J. "The Butterfly's World: Notes of a Butterfly Gardener." *University of Washington Arboretum Bulletin* 46, no. 2 (1983): 16–26.

Cribb, Peter. "How to Encourage Butterflies to Live in Your Garden." *Insect Conservation News* (Amateur Entomologists' Society, U.K.) 6 (1982): 4–10.

Damrosch, Barbara. "A Butterfly Garden." In *Theme Gardens*. New York: Workman, 1982.

Day, C. Burke, Jr. "Butterfly Paradise." *Saturday Evening Post* (July–August 1989).

Dimock, Thomas E. "Culture Maintenance of *Vanessa atalanta rubria* (Nymphalidae)." *The Journal of Research on the Lepidoptera* 23 (1984): 236–40.

Dirig, Robert. "Butterflies, Cabbages and Kids." *Teacher* (May–June 1976).

———. "Butterflies in Your Garden." *Grapevine* (September 4–10, 1986).

———. *Growing Moths*. 4-H Members' Guide no. M-6-6. Ithaca: New York State College of Agriculture and Life Sciences, Cornell University.

Donahue, Julian P. "How to Create a Butterfly Garden." *First Day Cover Page*. Pleasantville, N.Y., and Montreal: The Reader's Digest Association (1977).

———. "Take a Butterfly to Lunch: A Guide to Butterfly Gardening in Los Angeles." *Terra* 14, no. 3 (1976): 3–12 plus fold-out poster.

Druse, Ken. "Butterflies Are Free, but You Can Lure Them to Your Garden with Their Favorite Flowers." *House Beautiful* (August 1984).

Ginna, Robert Emmett, Jr. "A Shared Passion for Bugs." *Yankee* (September 1984).

Goodall, Nancy-Mary. "Flowers for Butterflies." *The Illustrated London News* (July 1978).

Green, Timothy. "Beautiful Fliers Fill an Indoor Jungle in Suburban London." *Smithsonian* (January 1985).

Grossman, Joel. "Planting a Butterfly Garden." *Flower and Garden* (April–May 1986): 60–61.

Haas, Carolyn, Ann Cole, and Barbara Naftzger. *Backyard Vacation: Outdoor Fun in Your Own Neighborhood*. Boston: Little, Brown, 1980.

Harrison, George H. "Boom Times for Backyard Habitat: How People Are Creating Havens for Wildlife in Their Own Backyards." *National Wildlife* (October–November 1983).

———. "A Farm Full of Butterflies." *Ranger Rick* (October 1982).

Hastings, Boyd. "Where Dandelions Grow." *Organic Gardening* (April 1981).

Headstrom, Richard. *Suburban Wildlife: An Introduction to the Common Animals of Your Back Yard and Local Park*. Englewood Cliffs, N.J.: Prentice-Hall, 1984.

Heal, Henry George. "An Experiment in Conservation Education: The Drum Manor Butterfly Garden." *International Journal of Environmental Studies* 4 (1973): 223–29.

Jackson, Bernard S. *Butterflies of Oxen Pond Botanic Park*. St. John's, Newfoundland: Memorial University of Newfoundland, 1976.

———. "Butterfly Farming in Newfoundland." *Canadian Geographic* (August–September 1979).

———. "How to Start a Butterfly Garden." *Nature Canada* (April–June 1977).

———. "The Lowly Dandelion Deserves More Respect." *Canadian Geographic* (June–July 1982).

———. "Oxen Pond Botanic Park." *Garden* (November–December 1981).

———. "The Red Admiral, the Mourning Cloak and the Painted Lady: How to Lure Them to Your Garden." *Nature Canada* (Summer 1987): 35.

Jimerson, Douglas A. "Welcome Butterflies: Plantings to Transform Your Yard into a Butterfly Paradise." *Better Homes and Gardens* (March 1987): 104–7.

Joode, Ton de, and Anthonie Stolk. "The Butterfly and the Moth." In *The Backyard Bestiary*. New York: Alfred A. Knopf, 1982.

Klinkenberg, Rose. "Wild About Lupines: Without Them, the Karner Blue Can't Survive." *Nature Canada* (Winter 1988): 10–11.

Kulman, H. M. "Butterfly Production Management." *University of Minnesota Agricultural Experiment Station Technical Bulletin* 310 (1977): 39–47.

Malinsky, Iris. "The Pleasure of Flowers and Butterflies." *Los Angeles Times, Home* (December 11, 1977).

Martin, Laura. "A Bit of Wilderness in Your Own Backyard." *National Wildlife* (April–May 1987): 22–28.

Measures, David G. "Butterflies in Your Garden." In *Bright Wings of Summer*. Englewood Cliffs, N.J.: Prentice-Hall, 1976.

Moran, B. K. "City Butterflies." *San Francisco* (April 1982).

Morton, Ashley. "The Importance of Farming Butterflies." *New Scientist* (May 20, 1982).

National Wildlife Federation. "Attracting Butterflies to Your Backyard Wildlife Habitat." In *Gardening with Wildlife*. Washington, D.C.: National Wildlife Federation, 1974.

Neulieb, Robert, and Marilyn Neulieb. "With Care, You Can Coax Butterflies into Residence." *Christian Science Monitor* (June 27, 1982): 15.

Newman, L. Hugh. "Churchill's Interest in Animal Life." *Audubon* (July–August 1965).

———. *Living With Butterflies*. London: John Baker, 1967.

———. "When Churchill Brought Butterflies to Chartwell." *Audubon* (May–June 1965).

Newman, L. Hugh, with Moira Savonius. *Create a Butterfly Garden*. London: John Baker, 1967.

Newson-Brighton, Maryanne. "A Garden of Butterflies." *Organic Gardening* (January 1983).

Norsgaard, E. Jaediker. "The Lawn That Went Wild." *Ranger Rick* (May–June 1976).

Oates, Matthew. *Garden Plants for Butterflies*. Fareham, Hampshire, England: Brian Masterson & Associates, 1985.

Opler, Paul A., and Whitney J. Cranshaw. "Attracting Butterflies to the Eastern Colorado Yard and Garden." *Service in Action*, no. 5504. Fort Collins: Colorado State University Cooperative Extension, 1986, 4 pp.

Oppewall, Jeannine. "History of Butterfly Farming in California." *Terra* 17, no. 4 (1979): 30–35.

Owen, Denis F. "Conservation of Butterflies in Garden Habitats." *Environmental Conservation* 3, no. 4 (1976): 285–90.

———. "Estimating the Abundance and Diversity of Butterflies." *Biological Conservation* 8 (1975): 173–83.

———. "Insect Diversity in an English Suburban Garden." In *Perspectives in Urban Entomology*. New York: Academic Press, 1978.

———. "Species Diversity in Butterflies in a Tropical Garden." *Biological Conservation* 3 (1971): 191–98.

Owen, Jennifer, and D. F. Owen. "Suburban Gardens: England's Most Important Nature Reserve?" *Environmental Conservation* 2, no. 1 (1975): 53–59.

Pyle, Robert Michael. "Butterfly Gardening." In *The Audubon Society Handbook for Butterfly Watchers*. New York: Charles Scribner's Sons, 1984.

———. "Create a Community Butterfly Reserve." *Xerces Society Self-Help Sheet No. 4*, 1975.

———. "Railways and Butterflies." *Xerces Society Self-Help Sheet No. 2*, 1974.

Reinhard, Harriet V. "Food Plants for Butterflies." *California Native Plant Society Newsletter* 6, no. 4 (1970): 3–6.

———. "Gardening for Butterflies." *Pacific Horticulture* 48, no. 4 (1987).

Rothschild, Miriam, and Clive Farrell. *The Butterfly Gardener*. London: Michael Joseph / Rainbird, 1983.

"She Raises Monarchs in Mid-Manhattan." *Smithsonian* (February 1979).

Simon, Seymour. "Butterflies and Moths." In *Pets in a Jar: Collecting and Caring for Small Wild Animals*. New York: Penguin Books, 1979.

Smith, Alice Upham. "Attracting Butterflies to the Garden." *Horticulture* (August 1975).

Smith, Jack. "A Passion for Butterflies." *Los Angeles Times, View* (April 13, 1976).

Snyder, Rachel. "Butterfly Gardens Are Soaring." *Flower and Garden* (March–April 1989): 50+.

Stokes, Bruce. "The Urban Garden: A Growing Trend." *Sierra* (July–August 1978).

Stone, John L. S., and H. J. Midwinter. *Butterfly Culture: A Guide to Breeding Butterflies, Moths, and Other Insects*. Poole, England: Blandford Press, 1975.

Tekulsky, Mathew. *The Butterfly Garden*. Boston: The Harvard Common Press, 1985.

———. "Butterfly Gardening." *Family Circle Great Ideas* (February 1983).

———. "Butterfly Goodbye." *Instructor* (May 1986).

Thomas, Jack Ward, Robert O. Brush, and Richard M. DeGraaf. "Invite Wildlife to Your Backyard." *National Wildlife* (April–May 1973). (Available as an updated reprint from the National Wildlife Federation, 1412 Sixteenth Street NW, Washington, DC 20036.)

Titlow, Debby Igleheart. "Gardens On the Wing." *Colorado Homes & Lifestyles* (May–June 1984).

Tylka, David. "Butterfly Gardens." *Missouri Conservationist* (June 1980).

Vietmeyer, Noel D. *Butterfly Farming in Papua New Guinea*. Washington, D.C.: National Academy Press, 1983.

———. "Butterfly Ranching Is Taking Wing in Papua New Guinea." *Smithsonian* (May 1979).

Villiard, Paul. *Moths and How to Rear Them*. New York: Funk & Wagnalls, 1969.

Weaver, Mary Anne. "Barely a Flutter at the World's First Walk-through Butterfly Zoo." *Christian Science Monitor* (February 22, 1985).

Williams, Ted. "A Butterfly Garden." *Garden* (July–August 1980).

———. "How to Plant a Butterfly Garden." *Sanctuary* (April 1984).

Wiltshire, Lilas. "Informal Garden Helps Lure Butterflies." *Los Angeles Times* (June 8, 1984): 1–A:6.

Wolf, Nancy, and Roger Guttentag. "Butterfly Season." *Eco-News* (May 1975).

Woodier, Olwen. "Luring Butterflies and Hummingbirds to Your Garden." *Woman's Day* (April 10, 1985).

Xerces Society. "Butterfly Gardening—One Way to Increase Urban Wildlife (California Edition)." *Xerces Society Educational Leaflet No. 2*, 1978.

Yajima, Minoru. "The Insectarium at Tama Zoo, Tokyo." *International Zoo Yearbook* 12 (1972): 96.

BUTTERFLY PHOTOGRAPHY

Allen, James. "How to Photograph Butterflies." *Terra* 23, no. 5 (1985): 25–30.

Blackford, William M. "Techniques in Butterfly Photography." *PSA Journal* (March 1986): 20–23.

Griffin, William D. "Winged Beauty." *PSA Journal* (April 1989): 26–29.

Lipske, Mike. "Letter Perfect: A Photographer Reviews His ABCs on the Spellbinding Wings of Butterflies." *National Wildlife* (February–March 1988): 12–13.

Meyer, Gladys L. "Moth and Butterfly Photography." *PSA Journal* (May 1989): 15–17.

Pyle, Robert Michael. *The Audubon Society Handbook for Butterfly Watchers: A Guide to Observing, Locating, Identifying, Studying, and Photographing Butterflies*. New York: Charles Scribner's Sons, 1984.

Shaw, John. "Splendor in the Grass: Tips from a Professional on How to Photograph Insects." *Blair & Ketchum's Country Journal* (June 1984).

Shin, Chin Fah. "Using a Butterfly Shooter: How You Can Get Good Shots of Butterflies and Other Flighty Subjects." *PSA Journal* (July 1987): 24–27.

Zuckerman, Jim. "Butterflies: They're Spectacular and They're Free!" *Petersen's Photographic Magazine* (June 1989): 54–58.

BUTTERFLY SHOWPLACES

Basveld, Jane. "Butterfly House." *Omni* (November 1985): 22–23.

Design News. "Butterflies Under Glass." *Design News* (October 17, 1988): 31–34.

Green, Timothy. "Beautiful Fliers Fill an Indoor Jungle in Suburban London." *Smithsonian* (January 1985): 114–18.

"Step into the World of Butterflies." *Southern Living* (May 1989).

FLOWERS AND GARDENING

Baker, Herbert G., and Paul D. Hurd, Jr. "Intrafloral Ecology." *Annual Review of Entomology* 13 (1968): 385–414.

Bloom, Alan. *Perennials for Your Garden*. New York: Charles Scribner's Sons, 1975.

Bock, Jane, and Yan Linhart, eds. *The Evolutionary Ecology of Plants*. Boulder, Colo.: West View Press, 1989.

Brickell, Christopher. *Pruning*. New York: Simon & Schuster, 1975.

Brockman, C. Frank. *Trees of North America*. New York: Golden Press, 1968.

Browse, Philip McMillan. *Plant Propagation*. New York: Simon & Schuster, 1988.

Bruce, Hal. *How to Grow Wildflowers and Wild Shrubs and Trees in Your Own Garden*. New York: Alfred A. Knopf, 1976.

Coombes, Allen J. *Dictionary of Plant Names*. Beaverton, Oreg.: Timber Press, 1985.

Crockett, James Underwood. *Annuals*. New York: Time-Life Books, 1973.

———. *Perennials*. New York: Time-Life Books, 1973.

Crockett, James Underwood, and Oliver E. Allen. *Wildflower Gardening*. Alexandria, Va.: Time-Life Books, 1977.

Damrosch, Barbara. *Theme Gardens*. New York: Workman, 1982.

Dennis, John V., and Matthew Kalmenoff. *The Wildlife Gardener*. New York: Alfred A. Knopf, 1985.

Faegri, K., and L. van der Pijl. *The Principles of Pollination Ecology*. Oxford, England: Pergamon Press, 1979.

Headstrom, Richard. *Suburban Wildflowers: An Introduction to the Common Wildflowers of Your Back Yard and Local Park*. Englewood Cliffs, N.J.: Prentice-Hall, 1984.

Hersey, Jean. *The Woman's Day Book of Wildflowers*. New York: Simon & Schuster, 1976.

Hobhouse, Penelope. *Color in Your Garden*. Boston: Little, Brown, 1985.

Johnson, Lady Bird, Carlton B. Lees, and Les Line. *Wildflowers Across America*. New York: Abbeville Press, 1988.

Kevan, Peter G. "Pollination and Environmental Conservation." *Environmental Conservation* 2, no. 4 (1975): 293–98.

Kruckeberg, Arthur R. *Gardening with Native Plants of the Pacific Northwest*. Seattle: University of Washington Press, 1982.

Lacy, Allen. "Butterfly Weed." In *Home Ground: A Gardener's Miscellany*. New York: Farrar, Straus & Giroux, 1984.

Niehaus, Theodore F. *A Field Guide to Pacific States Wildflowers*. Boston: Houghton Mifflin, 1976.

Niering, William A., and Nancy C. Olmstead. *The Audubon Society Field Guide to North American Wildflowers: Eastern Region*. New York: Alfred A. Knopf, 1979.

Peterson, Roger Tory, and Margaret McKenny. *A Field Guide to Wildflowers of Northeastern and North-Central North America*. Boston: Houghton Mifflin, 1968.

Proctor, Michael, and Peter Yeo. *The Pollination of Flowers*. London: Collins, 1973.

Ray, Mary Helen, and Robert P. Nicholls, eds. *A Guide to Significant & Historic Gardens of America*. Athens, Ga.: Agee, 1983.

Richards, A. J., ed. *The Pollination of Flowers by Insects*. Linnean Society Symposium Series, no. 6. London and Orlando, Fla.: Academic Press, 1978.

Ruggiero, Michael A. *Spotter's Guide to Wild Flowers of North America*. New York: Mayflower Books, 1979.

Sinnes, A. Cort. *All About Annuals*. San Francisco: Ortho Books, 1981.

———. *All About Perennials*. San Francisco: Ortho Books, 1981.

Spellenberg, Richard. *The Audubon Society Field Guide to North American Wildflowers: Western Region*. New York: Alfred A. Knopf, 1979.

Spencer, Edwin Rollin. *All About Weeds*. New York: Dover, 1974.

Sperka, Marie. *Growing Wildflowers: A Gardener's Guide*. New York: Charles Scribner's Sons, 1984.

Steffek, Edwin F. *The New Wild Flowers and How to Grow Them*. Beaverton, Oreg.: Timber Press, 1983.

Sunset Books. *Color in Your Garden*. Menlo Park, Calif.: Lane, 1975.

———. *Sunset Western Garden Book*. Menlo Park, Calif.: Lane, 1988.

Taylor, Kathryn S., and Stephen F. Hamblin. *Handbook of Wild Flower Cultivation*. New York: Macmillan, 1963.

Tenenbaum, Frances. *Gardening with Wild Flowers*. New York: Charles Scribner's Sons, 1973.

Tufts, Craig. *The Backyard Naturalist*. Washington, D.C.: National Wildlife Federation, 1988.

United States Department of Agriculture. *Common Weeds of the United States*. New York: Dover, 1971.

Verey, Rosemary. *The Scented Garden*. New York: Van Nostrand Reinhold, 1981.

Weber, William A. *Rocky Mountain Flora*. Boulder: Colorado Associated University Press, 1976.

Wyman, Donald. *Shrubs and Vines for American Gardens*. Rev. ed. New York: Macmillan, 1974.

———. *Trees for American Gardens*. Rev. ed. New York: Macmillan, 1965.

Master Plant List
Photographic Credits

Page 84: *Abelia* × *grandiflora* (glossy abelia).   NANCY A. DAWE
Achillea filipendulina (fernleaf yarrow).   CRANDALL & CRANDALL

Page 85: *Asclepias tuberosa* (butterfly weed).   IRENE VANDERMOLEN,
BRUCE COLEMAN, INC.
Aster × *frikartii* (Frikart aster).   NANCY A. DAWE
Buddleia davidii (butterfly bush, summer lilac).   MARY JANE HAYES

Page 86: *Centranthus ruber* (Jupiter's-beard, red valerian).   JERRY PAVIA
Chrysanthemum × *superbum* (Shasta daisy).   CRANDALL & CRANDALL
Cosmos bipinnatus (cosmos).   NANCY A. DAWE
Echinacea purpurea (purple coneflower).   NANCY A. DAWE

Page 87: *Eupatorium* sp. (Joe-Pye-weed).   DON RIEPE
Helianthus sp. (sunflower).   CRANDALL & CRANDALL
Heliotropium arborescens (heliotrope, cherry-pie).   JERRY PAVIA

Page 88: *Hemerocallis* sp. (daylily).   JOANNE PAVIA
Lantana camara (lantana, yellow sage).   CRANDALL & CRANDALL
Lavandula angustifolia (lavender, English lavender). *Rudbeckia* is also
shown.   JOANNE PAVIA

Page 89: *Liatris spicata* (spike gayfeather, spike blazing-star).   NANCY A. DAWE
Ligustrum japonicum (wax-leaf privet, Japanese privet).
CRANDALL & CRANDALL
Lonicera japonica (Japanese honeysuckle).   MARY JANE HAYES

Page 90: *Mentha* × *piperita* (peppermint).   NANCY A. DAWE

Monarda didyma (bee balm, Oswego tea).
E. R. DEGGINGER, BRUCE COLEMAN, INC.

Nicotiana alata (flowering tobacco).   CRANDALL & CRANDALL

Petunia × *hybrida* (common garden petunia).   NANCY A. DAWE

Page 91: *Phlox paniculata* (garden phlox, summer phlox, hardy phlox).
MARY JANE HAYES

Rosmarinus officinalis (rosemary).   JOANNE PAVIA

Rudbeckia hirta (gloriosa daisy).   NANCY A. DAWE

Page 92: *Scabiosa caucasica* (pincushion flower).   JOANNE PAVIA

Sedum spectabile (showy stonecrop).   CRANDALL & CRANDALL

Solidago canadensis (goldenrod).   JOANNE PAVIA

Page 93: *Tagetes patula* (French marigold), 'Honeycomb' variety.
JOANNE PAVIA

Zinnia elegans (common zinnia).   JERRY PAVIA

INDEX

~

This index lists all butterflies, moths, and plants mentioned or illustrated in the text; entries are by Latin name and any common names cited in the text.

Abelia, 75
Abelia × grandiflora, 84
Achillea filipendulina, 81, 84
Achillea filipendulina 'Coronation Gold', 77
Actias luna, 102
Ageratum, 79
Agraulis vanillae, 3, 4, 26, 35, 119
Alfalfa, 63
American painted lady, 30, 57
American tent caterpillar, 31
Anartia jatrophae, 13
Anglewings, 32, 39, 66
Anise swallowtail, 66
Apocynum cannabinum, 108
Araujia sericifera, 45
Argiope aurantia, 37
Arizona poppy, 113
Arugula, 72
Asclepias, 120
Asclepias incarnata, 56, 85
Asclepias speciosa, 85
Asclepias tuberosa, 77, 81, 85
Ash, 9
Aster × frikartii, 85
Aster novae-angliae, 85
Aster novi-belgii, 85
Asters, 59, 79
Atlides halesus, 106

Baltimores, 57–58
Banded purple, 41
Battus philenor, 2
Bay checkerspot, 3

Bee balm, 66, 72, 79, 81, 90
Beech, 31
Bermuda grass, 83
Bidens pilosa, 5
Bittersweet, 9
Blackberries, 83
Black-eyed Susan, 77, 81, 91
Black swallowtails, 28, 30, 32, 58, 59, 66
Black walnut, 31
Bladder flower, 45
Bluebell woods, 20–21
Blueberry, 101
Blues, 9, 32, 39
Boneset, 57
Brassica oleracea, 50
Broccoli, 63
Brussels sprouts, 63
Bryonies, 9
Buckeye, 118
Buck moth, 33, 38
Buddleia, 10, 11, 12
Buddleia davidii, 81, 85
Buttercups, 9
Butterfly bush, 12, 72, 75, 81
Butterfly weed, 66, 77, 81, 85

Cabbage, 43, 50, 63
Cabbage butterflies, 66
Cabbage white, 32, 66, 72
Calephelis virginiensis, 22
Callophrys viridis, 116
Callosamia, 30
Candytuft, 9